The Wisdom for Creating Happiness and Peace

Selections From the Works of Daisaku Ikeda

The WISDOM for CREATING HAPPINESS and PEACE

SELECTIONS FROM THE WORKS OF

Daisaku Ikeda

Part 1: Happiness

Published by World Tribune Press
A division of the SGI-USA
606 Wilshire Blvd.
Santa Monica, CA 90401

Printed in the United States of America.

Cover and interior design by Gopa & Ted2, Inc.

10 9 8 7 6 5 4 3 2 1

ISBN: 978-1-935523-76-5

Library of Congress Control Number: 2015949377

Contents

Editor's Note

THIS FIRST PART of "The Wisdom for Creating Happiness and Peace" was serialized in the *Living Buddhism* magazine from July 2014 to March 2015.

The citations most commonly used in this book have been abbreviated as follows:

LSOC, page number(s) refers to *The Lotus Sutra and Its Opening and Closing Sutras*, translated by Burton Watson (Tokyo: Soka Gakkai, 2009).

OTT, page number(s) refers to *The Record of the Orally Transmitted Teachings*, translated by Burton Watson (Tokyo: Soka Gakkai, 2004).

WND, page number(s) refers to *The Writings of Nichiren Daishonin*, vol. 1 (WND-1) (Tokyo: Soka Gakkai, 1999) and vol. 2 (WND-2) (Tokyo: Soka Gakkai: 2006).

Editor's Note to Original Series

THIS YEAR MARKS the fifty-fourth anniversary of SGI President Daisaku Ikeda's inauguration as the third president of the Soka Gakkai on May 3, 1960. That day can also be seen as the start of his journey to spread Nichiren Buddhism around the world. It has been a journey rooted in his commitment to actualize the cherished wish of his mentor, the second Soka Gakkai president, Josei Toda, to rid the world of misery.

President Ikeda has dedicated himself for more than five decades to the realization of world peace and the happiness of humanity. Due to these efforts, and those of countless fellow members who have joined him in this endeavor, the harmonious, humanistic network of the SGI has spread to 192 countries and territories.

He has spoken and written tirelessly to bring courage and hope to those weighed down by suffering and sorrow. His words are a source of boundless inspiration, brimming with the passion and energy of a great philosopher of action. In testament to his prodigious output, the Japanese edition of his collected writings, *Ikeda Daisaku zenshu* (The Collected Writings of Daisaku Ikeda), will soon reach 150 volumes.

At the start of this new era of worldwide kosen-rufu, we have compiled a selection of excerpts from President Ikeda's guidance, consisting mainly of passages from his collected works. This compilation will be serialized under the title *The Wisdom for Creating*

Happiness and Peace. Translations in various languages will also be produced so that the many new members emerging around the globe can study President Ikeda's thought and philosophy.

The excerpts selected for this new series have been organized into three parts:

Part 1. Happiness
Part 2. Human Revolution
Part 3. Kosen-rufu and World Peace

Part 1—"Happiness"—will discuss the differences between relative and absolute happiness; the teaching of the Ten Worlds as a principle for transforming our lives; the significance of carrying out the daily practice of gongyo and chanting daimoku for effecting that transformation; and the Buddhist view of life and death, in which both are experienced with joy.

Part 2—"Human Revolution"—will focus on the Buddhist way of life, in which people strive to bring forth their highest potential and shine with courage, wisdom, and compassion.

Part 3—"Kosen-rufu and World Peace"—will take up the ideals and principles of worldwide kosen-rufu; the movement and humanistic organization of the SGI; the spirit of the oneness of mentor and disciple shared by the first three Soka Gakkai presidents, Tsunesaburo Makiguchi, Josei Toda, and Daisaku Ikeda; world peace; and respect for the dignity of life.

The start of each chapter and each selected excerpt within that chapter will be prefaced with a brief introductory explanation to clarify important points. At the end of each excerpt, we will include source details—for example, in the case of speeches, the occasion, place, and date—as a reference for further study.

It is also to be noted that President Ikeda's speeches are always tailored to his audience, addressing the issues that people are facing at that time or in that country, rather than serving as systematic, step-by-step presentations of Buddhism. At the same time, however, they also express a universal message, transcending any particular time or place.

With the approval of President Ikeda, we have made some minor edits and revisions to the selected excerpts to convey his message to readers around the world more clearly and accessibly. In the case of those excerpts that were originally in dialogue format, President Ikeda's remarks have been recast as monologues to read more naturally.

We hope that this series will serve as an opportunity for readers to learn from the wisdom contained in President Ikeda's great body of work, thereby lending support to the movement of human revolution dedicated to the happiness of all people and the realization of world peace.

Selected Excerpts Editorial Committee
April 2014

CHAPTER 1
What Is True Happiness?

Introduction to the Chapter:

All of us are searching for happiness in life, but what constitutes happiness is different for each person. Among all the different kinds of happiness, is there a true happiness that offers complete fulfillment to all?

This chapter examines the differences between relative and absolute happiness.

Fulfilling desires for such things as wealth, fame, or social standing constitutes relative happiness. These desires know no limit. Even if we gain such worldly benefits, they are ultimately insubstantial and ephemeral. Their allure can fade in an instant when we compare them with what others may have. And when they fail to deliver the anticipated satisfaction, we may regret ever having pursued them in the first place. If we seek only relative happiness, we cannot build a truly happy life.

In contrast, absolute happiness is attained by developing a state of life characterized by a powerful life force and rich wisdom that enable us to overcome any kind of suffering and adversity—a state of being in which living itself is a joy. Attaining absolute happiness is a fundamental goal for all.

Nichiren Daishonin, born in thirteenth-century Japan, established a means by which all human beings can bring forth their inherent Buddhahood, the supreme state of life, and thereby attain absolute happiness. Today, the SGI is dynamically spreading the Nichiren Buddhism on a global scale.

Based on the concept of absolute happiness discussed in this chapter, the chapters that follow will present in concrete terms the principles and means for inner transformation.

1.1 Faith for Absolute Happiness

How can we live the very best life? Nichiren Buddhism offers a clear and comprehensible answer to this fundamental question. Nichiren Daishonin awakened to the Mystic Law and expressed it in the form of the Gohonzon, the object of devotion, to enable all people to attain happiness. In this excerpt, President Ikeda teaches the importance of seeking absolute happiness, which is indestructible and characterized by supreme joy, wisdom, and compassion, rather than relative happiness, which is destined to fade and disappear with time. In addition, referring to the Buddhist view of the eternity of life, President Ikeda emphasizes that when we chant with unwavering faith in the Gohonzon and bring forth boundless life force from within, we can transform in this present lifetime negative karma we have accumulated in the past and achieve absolute happiness that will continue into the future.

■ "How do I live my life?" "How can I live the very best life?"—these are fundamental questions. How to live is an inescapable issue that confronts all who are born in this world, one that has been pursued by countless philosophies, ideologies, and religions. At the most basic level, politics, economics, and science, too, are inseparable from this issue. Their original purpose is to help people live the happiest of lives. None of these areas of human endeavor, however, can provide an answer to the question "What constitutes the best life?" They have no clear or conclusive answer that is rationally convincing.

Buddhism supplies a coherent answer to this question. Shakyamuni Buddha, the Great Teacher T'ien-t'ai, and Nichiren Daishonin each set forth a clear response. In particular, the conclusions of Shakyamuni and Nichiren are exactly the same.

Moreover, based on his conclusion, Nichiren left behind a concrete "tool" that all people can use to become happy. He bestowed the Gohonzon—which the second Soka Gakkai president, Josei Toda, referred to as a "happiness-producing device"—upon all humankind.

What is the definition of human happiness? There is a Thai saying, "False happiness makes people become haughty and arrogant. Real happiness makes people joyful and fills them with wisdom and compassion."[1]

Is one happy just because one is wealthy? All too many people have allowed money to ruin their lives.

President Toda stressed the importance of absolute happiness over relative happiness. Absolute happiness is not how one stands compared with others, nor is it a transitory, illusory happiness that fades with the passing of time. Mr. Toda taught that we practice Nichiren Buddhism to attain a state of life where, no matter what circumstances we may encounter, we can feel that life itself is a joy. When we attain that state of life, our lives overflow with unsurpassed joy, wisdom, and compassion—just as the Thai proverb says, "Real happiness makes people joyful and fills them with wisdom and compassion."

The Daishonin states, "Both oneself and others together will take joy in their possession of wisdom and compassion" (OTT, 146). Our practice of Nichiren Buddhism and our organization for kosen-rufu exist so that we, and also others, may attain absolute happiness.

All kinds of things happen in life. There is sorrow, there is suffering. Every day, there are things we may find unpleasant or annoying. Married couples may sometimes quarrel, and some may go through painful divorces. Even if a couple does get along well, they may have a sick child, or one of them may suffer illness. We face all kinds of sufferings and problems. How formidable are the challenges of living!

Faith is the engine that enables us to persevere in life to the very end. Our Buddhist practice serves as the propulsive force for piercing through the clouds of suffering like a rocket and powerfully ascending higher and higher, without limit, to fly serenely through the skies of happiness.

When we chant Nam-myoho-renge-kyo, hope and the strength to always live positively surge within us. Buddhism teaches that earthly desires—deluded impulses that are a cause of suffering—can be a springboard to enlightenment. Through faith in the Mystic Law, we can develop the ability to change all that is negative in our lives into something positive. We can transform all problems into happiness, sufferings into joy, anxiety into hope, and worry into peace of mind. We can always find a way forward.

Nichiren writes, "*Myo* [of *myoho,* the Mystic Law] means to revive, that is, to return to life" (WND-1, 149). It is the immense power of the Mystic Law that gives vitality to and breathes fresh life into all things, including individuals, organizations, societies, and nations.

As human beings, we also possess our own unique karma. You may wish you had been born into a wealthier family, but the reality is that you weren't. Or you may wish you were better looking—but, of course, that doesn't apply to anyone here in Thailand! You are all so beautiful. Anyway, these are just some examples, and there are many other areas where karma comes into play. Essentially, the concept of karma can be understood only when viewed from the perspective of life's eternity over the three existences of past, present, and future. There are past existences and the law of cause and effect to take into account.

And these past existences may not necessarily all have been on this planet. Many in astronomy and related fields today think that, given the enormously vast numbers of stars and planets in the known universe, other intelligent life forms similar to human beings must exist.

In any case, our present reality is that we have been born here on Earth. This is an inalterable fact. How can we discover our true path? How can we change our karma and build a truly wonderful and meaningful existence? The answer is, in short, by embracing faith in the Mystic Law. Through our practice of Nichiren Buddhism, we can change any negative karma and transform the place where we are into the Land of Tranquil Light, a place overflowing with happiness.

Moreover, Nichiren Buddhism focuses on the present and the future. By always moving forward from this moment on, we can develop our lives boundlessly. We can also open up infinite possibilities for our next life and lifetimes after that. We can reveal the immeasurable treasures within us and make our lives shine with the full brilliance of those treasures. Such is the power of practicing Nichiren Buddhism.

From a speech delivered at the 1st Soka Gakkai Thailand General Meeting, Soka Gakkai Thailand Culture Center, Bangkok, February 6, 1994.

1.2 Absolute Happiness and Relative Happiness

The founding Soka Gakkai President, Tsunesaburo Makiguchi, said, "The purpose of life is to create supreme value and to attain the greatest possible happiness." President Toda said, "Absolute happiness means that being alive itself is a joy." In this selection, based on those insights, President Ikeda underscores that the SGI is an organization dedicated to helping people attain the greatest possible happiness—absolute happiness.

■ What is the purpose of life? It is happiness. The goal of Buddhism and of faith, too, is to become happy.

Nichiren writes: "There is no true happiness for human beings other than chanting Nam-myoho-renge-kyo. The [Lotus Sutra] reads, '. . . where living beings enjoy themselves at ease'" (WND-1, 681). "Enjoy themselves at ease" here means being freely able to live the kind of life one desires and wholeheartedly enjoying that life.

If you possess strong life force and abundant wisdom, it is possible to enjoy the challenge of overcoming life's hardships much in the same way that waves make surfing exhilarating and steep mountains give mountaineering its appeal.

Because the Mystic Law is the source of the life force and wisdom for overcoming life's difficulties, the Daishonin states that there is no greater happiness than chanting Nam-myoho-renge-kyo.

Reality is harsh. Please courageously challenge the stern realities of life and win, and win again, in everything—in daily life, work, school, and family relations. The teachings of Buddhism and our practice of faith are the driving force for unlimited improvement.

Where people possess wisdom and life force derived from their Buddhist practice, they can move everything in a brighter, more positive, and more encouraging direction. Wise, genuine practitioners of Nichiren Buddhism can enter into a winning rhythm in actuality, not just in theory.

President Toda gave the following guidance on happiness:

> I would like to say a few words about happiness. There are two kinds of happiness: absolute happiness and relative happiness. Absolute happiness is attaining Buddhahood. . . . Relative happiness means that your everyday wishes are fulfilled one by one—for instance, to have a million yen, a wonderful spouse, fine children, a nice house or clothes, and so on. . . . Such happiness is not of great consequence. Yet everyone is convinced that this is what being happy is all about.
>
> What, then, is absolute happiness? Absolute happiness means that being alive and here itself is a joy. . . . It also implies a state where one is free of financial worries and enjoys adequate good health, where there is peace and harmony in one's family and one's business prospers, and where all that one sees and hears brings one a wonderful sense of pleasure and joy. When we achieve such a state of life, this world, this strife-ridden saha world, will itself become a pure land. This is what we call attaining the state of Buddhahood. . . .
>
> How can we achieve this? We must shift from the pursuit of relative happiness to that of absolute happiness. Only our practice of Nichiren Buddhism can make this happen. I'm working furiously to share this truth with others; so I hope you will have utter confidence in my words and lead such lives [of absolute happiness].[2]

President Makiguchi once said: "There are some people who go around saying, 'I saved the money I wanted, bought the house

I wanted, so now I can sit back, enjoy a drink, and indulge in a few luxuries. What more can I want in life than that?' This kind of person has no understanding of the true purpose of life." On this point, Mr. Makiguchi clearly stated, "The purpose of life is to create supreme value and to attain the greatest happiness."

The name Soka Gakkai (literally "Value Creation Society") means an organization whose members are committed to creating supreme value and attaining the greatest happiness.

The purpose of life is to realize this kind of happiness, in other words, absolute happiness. Absolute happiness is something that doesn't change with time; it is eternal and unaffected by external factors, welling forth from the depths of one's life. It is not a transitory thing like worldly status and fortune or some other fleeting satisfaction.

What matters is living in accord with the Law and attaining an elevated state of life based on the Law. The state of life we attain, like the Law itself, is eternal. As practitioners of Nichiren Buddhism, we can make our way as champions of life throughout eternity.

Some people say that happiness is just a state of mind and that if you think you're happy you will be, even if you're suffering from illness or poverty. But if it's just something you're telling yourself without actually feeling any real sense of happiness in the depths of your being, then it's ultimately meaningless.

The "treasures of the heart" that we accumulate through our practice of Nichiren Buddhism will manifest in our lives over time as "treasures of the body" and "treasures of the storehouse" (see WND-1, 851).

Every day, I am earnestly praying that you may enjoy comfortable lives, good health, and longevity. And I will continue to pray wholeheartedly for this as long as I live. It is my ardent wish that each of you will fulfill all of your heart's desires, so that you can declare in your closing days: "My life has been a happy one. I have no regrets. It has been a satisfying life."

From a speech delivered at the Rio de Janeiro General Meeting, Rio de Janeiro Culture Center, Brazil, February 13, 1993.

1.3 Becoming Happy Where We Are Right Now

People tend to think of happiness as existing somewhere or sometime beyond their present circumstances. But true happiness exists in the here and now and is realized by pressing forward with hope in our ongoing struggles with daily realities. In this selection, President Ikeda discusses the attitude in faith we need in order to transform the place where we are now into a place of victory and happiness.

■ In *The Record of the Orally Transmitted Teachings,* Nichiren Daishonin explains the following passage from "Encouragements of the Bodhisattva Universal Worthy," the twenty-eighth chapter of the Lotus Sutra: "Before long this person will proceed to the place of practice" (LSOC, 364), stating:

> The words "this person" refer to the practitioner of the Lotus Sutra. The place where the person upholds and honors the Lotus Sutra is the "place of practice" to which the person proceeds. It is not that he leaves his present place and goes to some other place. The "place of practice" is the place where the living beings of the Ten Worlds reside.

> And now the place where Nichiren and his followers chant Nam-myoho-renge-kyo, "whether . . . in mountain valleys or the wide wilderness" [LSOC, 316], these places are all the Land of Eternally Tranquil Light. This is what is meant by the "place of practice." (see OTT, 192)[3]

"This person" refers to the practitioner, or votary, of the Lotus Sutra. In the specific sense, it indicates Nichiren himself, while in the more general sense, it refers to all people who embrace and practice Nam-myoho-renge-kyo of the Three Great Secret Laws. The place where people embrace and practice the correct teaching of Buddhism is the "'place of practice' to which the person proceeds," in other words, the place where we strive to attain Buddhahood in this lifetime.

There is no need to leave this trouble-filled saha world for some otherworldly pure land or ideal paradise. The "place of practice" is none other than the dwelling place of living beings of the Ten Worlds. Now, the place where Nichiren and his disciples who chant Nam-myoho-renge-kyo reside is the land of Eternally Tranquil Light, or the Buddha land, whether it be "in mountain valleys or the wide wilderness" (LSOC, 316). It is the "place of practice," Nichiren asserts. The place where each practitioner lives becomes the Land of Tranquil Light. This passage alludes to the profound transformative power inherent in a single life moment.

People often tend to think of happiness as something abstract and removed from their present realities. They imagine, for example, that they would be happier if they could move to another place, or that they would enjoy more comfortable and pleasant lives if they could change jobs. They always feel that the grass is greener on the other side and place their hopes on a change of external circumstances. Young people are particularly susceptible to this tendency.

However, we all have different missions to fulfill in life and different places where we need to live to fulfill them. Those who decide to put down solid roots where they are and continue to live their lives with perseverance and hope while struggling with reality will be victors in life. It's important not to live aimlessly, lacking any clear purpose. I therefore say to you: "Dig beneath your feet, there you will find a spring," and "Live in a way that is true to yourself."

In short, a real sense of happiness and deep satisfaction in life can be found only within us. The Mystic Law is the fundamental Law of life. Through our Buddhist practice, we can tap the power of the Mystic Law to propel our lives forward. This is why the place where we carry out our Buddhist practice and society itself become the Buddha land. We are able to transform where we live right now into a place of victory and happiness.

From a speech delivered at the University Groups and Toshima Ward Joint Training Session, Soka Culture Center, Shinanomachi, Tokyo, December 7, 1986.

1.4 Happiness Lies Within Us

In this excerpt, President Ikeda stresses that all people possess within them an eternal and indestructible "palace of happiness." This is our Buddhahood. Yet, all too many people seek their "palace of happiness" in such things as wealth, fame, and social standing. By opening the "palace" of Buddhahood within us through our Buddhist practice, however, we can secure both material and spiritual happiness.

■ Where is the palace of happiness, the indestructible bastion of happiness that so many are eagerly seeking? And how is it to be acquired?

In *The Record of the Orally Transmitted Teachings,* Nichiren states, "Chanting Nam-myoho-renge-kyo is what is meant by entering the palace of oneself" (OTT, 209).

The indestructible life state of Buddhahood exists within us all. It could be described as an everlasting palace of happiness, adorned with countless glittering treasures. By embracing faith in the Mystic Law and chanting Nam-myoho-renge-kyo, we can enter this palace within our lives. In other words, the Daishonin teaches that we have the capacity to make the "palace of oneself" shine with supreme brilliance.

People seek all kinds of worldly "palaces of happiness." Some seek wealth or social standing, while others wish for fame, celebrity, or popularity. But none of those things have the permanence of a steadfast mountain peak. In our ever-changing existences, they are like the light of fireflies, flickering beautifully but destined to fade and disappear all too soon.

A life spent in pursuit of the ephemeral, transitory glories of the world is also ephemeral and transitory. Chasing eagerly after forms of happiness that are insubstantial and impermanent is a sad and empty way to live.

As Nichiren says, one's own highest state of life is an eternal and indestructible palace, a true bastion of happiness.

People may live in fine houses or possess great wealth, but if their hearts are mean and their life conditions are low, they will not be truly happy; they will be dwelling in palaces of misery. In contrast, people who have beautiful, generous hearts and a high life condition, irrespective of their present circumstances, are certain to attain both material and spiritual happiness. This accords with the Buddhist principle of the oneness of life and its environment—that our lives and our surroundings are one and inseparable.

When we open the palace of our own lives, it will eventually lead to the "palace of happiness" opening in others' lives and the "palace of prosperity" opening in society. There is an underlying continuity between the process of opening one's own palace and others doing likewise. This is a wonderful principle of Buddhism.

In today's complex society, where it is all too easy to succumb to negative influences, the wisdom to live mindfully and meaningfully is crucial. Our Buddhist practice enables us to open up our lives and become happy. By continuing to develop and deepen our faith and wisdom, we can become true champions as human beings and ongoing victors in the journey of life.

Supreme happiness is savored by those who, through practicing Nichiren Buddhism, make the palace of their lives shine eternally throughout the three existences of past, present, and future.

You are each building and opening your own palace of happiness day by day through your activities for kosen-rufu. You are certain, as a result, to attain Buddhahood in this lifetime and to become noble champions of happiness dwelling in a great palace of life as vast as the universe itself. I hope you will continue forging ahead on the great path of faith with confidence and optimism, filled with strong conviction and pride.

From a speech delivered at the 1st Nagano Prefecture General Meeting, Nagano Training Center, Karuizawa, Japan, August 12, 1990.

1.5 The Six Conditions for Happiness

This selection considers the nature of relative happiness and absolute happiness, offering six concrete conditions for happiness: fulfillment, a profound philosophy, conviction, cheer and vibrancy, courage, and tolerance. All six of these conditions are encompassed in faith in the Mystic Law. A life dedicated to practicing Nichiren Buddhism is one of supreme happiness.

■ In his writings, Nichiren states, "You must not spend your lives in vain and regret it for ten thousand years to come" (WND-1, 622).

How should we live our lives? What is the most valuable and worthwhile way to live? A well-known Japanese poem goes: "The life of a flower is short / Sufferings only are there many."[4] The meaning of these lines is that flowers suddenly come into bloom and then, just as suddenly, their petals fall and scatter; ultimately, the only thing that lasts for a long time is suffering. Life, indeed, may be like that in some ways.

A philosopher once remarked that perhaps the only way to determine happiness or unhappiness in life is by adding up, at the end of one's days, all the joys and all the sorrows one has experienced and basing one's final evaluation on whichever figure was larger.

Despite having illustrious positions in society or great material wealth, there are many people who fail to become happy. Despite enjoying wonderfully happy marriages or relationships, people must ultimately be parted from the person they love through death. Being separated from loved ones is one of the unavoidable sufferings inherent in the human condition. There are many who, despite gaining great fame and popularity, die after long, agonizing illnesses. Despite being born with exceptional beauty, not a few have been brought to misery by this seeming advantage.

Where is happiness to be found? How can we become happy? These are fundamental questions of life, and human beings are no doubt destined to pursue them eternally. The teachings of Nichiren Buddhism and faith in the Mystic Law provide fundamental answers to these questions.

Ultimately, happiness rests on our establishing a solid sense of self. Happiness based on such externals as possessing a fine house or a good reputation is "relative happiness." It is not a firm, unchanging "absolute happiness." Some might seem to be in the most fortunate circumstances, but if they feel only emptiness and pain, then they cannot be considered happy.

Some people live in truly splendid houses yet do nothing but fight in them. Some people work for famous companies and enjoy a prestige that many envy yet are always being shouted at by their superiors, left exhausted from heavy workloads, and feel no sense of joy or fulfillment in life.

Happiness does not lie in outward appearances or in vanity. It is a matter of what we feel inside; it is a deep resonance in our lives. I would venture, therefore, that the first condition for happiness is fulfillment.

To be filled each day with a rewarding sense of exhilaration and purpose, a sense of tasks accomplished, and deep fulfillment—people who feel this way are happy. Those who have this sense of satisfaction even if they are extremely busy are much happier than those who have free time on their hands but feel empty inside.

As practitioners of Nichiren Buddhism, we get up in the morning and do gongyo. Some perhaps may do so rather reluctantly! Nevertheless, doing gongyo is itself a truly great and noble thing. Gongyo is a solemn ceremony in which we are, in a manner of speaking, gazing out across the universe; it is a dialogue with the universe.

Reciting the sutra and chanting before the Gohonzon represent the dawn, the start of a new day, in our lives; it is the sun rising; it gives us a profound sense of contentment in the depths of our being that nothing can surpass. Even on this point alone, we are truly fortunate.

Some people appear to be happy but actually start off the day feeling depressed. A husband might be admonished by his wife in the morning and begin his day dejected, wondering, "How on earth did I get into such a marriage?" He will savor neither happiness nor contentment. Just by looking at our mornings, it is clear that we in the SGI lead lives of profound worth and satisfaction.

In addition, each of you is striving to do your best in your job or other responsibilities and to win in all areas of life while using your spare time to work for Buddhism, kosen-rufu, people's happiness, and the welfare of society. In this Latter Day of the Law teeming with perverse individuals, you are exerting yourselves energetically, often amid many hardships and obstacles, chanting for others' happiness, traveling long distances to talk with friends and show them warm concern and understanding. You are truly bodhisattvas. There is no nobler life, no life based on a loftier philosophy. Each of you is translating this unsurpassed philosophy into action and spreading its message far and wide. To possess a philosophy of such profound value is itself the greatest fortune. Accordingly, the second condition for happiness is to possess a profound philosophy.

The third condition for happiness is to possess conviction. We live in an age in which people can no longer clearly distinguish what is right or wrong, good or evil. This is a global trend. If things continue in this way, humanity is destined for chaos and moral decay. In the midst of such times, you are upholding and earnestly practicing Nichiren Buddhism, a teaching of the highest good.

In "The Opening of the Eyes," the Daishonin writes: "This I will state. Let the gods forsake me. Let all persecutions assail me. Still I will give my life for the sake of the Law" (WND-1, 280). In this same letter, he instructs his believers not to be swayed by temptations or threats, however great—such as being offered the rulership of Japan or being told that one's parents will be beheaded (see WND-1, 280).

The important thing is holding on resolutely to one's convictions, come what may, just as Nichiren teaches. People who possess such unwavering conviction will definitely become happy. Each of you is such an individual.

The fourth condition is living cheerfully and vibrantly. Those who are always complaining and grumbling make not only themselves but everyone else around them miserable and unhappy. By contrast, those who always live positively and filled with enthusiasm—those who possess a cheerful and sunny disposition that lifts the spirits and brightens the hearts of everyone they meet—are not only happy themselves but are a source of hope and inspiration for others.

Those who are always wearing long, gloomy expressions whenever you meet them and who have lost the ability to rejoice and feel genuine delight or wonder lead dark, cheerless existences.

On the other hand, those who possess good cheer can view even a scolding by a loved one, such as a spouse or partner, as sweet music to their ears, or they can greet a child's poor report card as a sign of great potential for improvement! Viewing events and situations in this kind of positive light is important. The strength, wisdom, and cheerfulness that accompany such an attitude lead to happiness.

To regard everything in a positive light or with a spirit of goodwill, however, does not mean being foolishly gullible and allowing people to take advantage of our good nature. It means having the wisdom and perception to actually move things in a positive direction by seeing things in their best light, while all the time keeping our eyes firmly focused on reality.

Faith and the teachings of Buddhism enable us to develop that kind of character. The acquisition of such character is a more priceless treasure than any other possession in life.

The fifth condition for happiness is courage. Courageous people can overcome anything. The cowardly, on the other hand, because of their lack of courage, fail to savor the true, profound joys of life. This is most unfortunate.

The sixth condition for happiness is tolerance. Those who are tolerant and broad-minded make people feel comfortable and at ease. Narrow and intolerant people who berate others for the slightest thing or who make a great commotion each time some problem arises just exhaust and intimidate everyone. Leaders, in particular, must absolutely not intimidate or exhaust others. They must be tolerant and have a warm approachability that makes people feel relaxed and comfortable. Not only are those who possess a heart as wide as the ocean happy themselves, but all those around them are happy too.

The six conditions I have just mentioned are all ultimately encompassed in the single word *faith.* A life based on faith in the Mystic Law is a life of unsurpassed happiness.

The Daishonin writes, "Nam-myoho-renge-kyo is the greatest of all joys" (OTT, 212). I hope all of you will savor the truth of these words deep in your lives and show vibrant actual proof of that joy.

From a speech delivered at the 21st SGI General Meeting, Florida Nature and Culture Center, Florida, USA, June 23, 1996.

CHAPTER 2

The Principle for Transforming Our Lives

Introduction to the Chapter:

As discussed in chapter 1, it is important to seek absolute happiness over relative happiness. How, then, do we go about achieving it? Absolute happiness is not something that is given to us. Based on the principles of Nichiren Buddhism, SGI President Ikeda explains that it can only be attained through our personal inner transformation.

Our lives possess a wide range of possibilities; they can move in a positive or a negative direction, toward either happiness or unhappiness. We may at times find ourselves in the depths of suffering or at the mercy of our desires and instinctual urges. At other times, we may feel calm and content with our lives or feel motivated by compassion to reach out and help those who are suffering.

Buddhism explores these various potential conditions, categorizing them into ten states of life called the Ten Worlds. Among the Ten Worlds, the world of Buddhahood accords with our noblest potential and highest state of life.

Nichiren identified the Law permeating the universe and life as Nam-myoho-renge-kyo and embodied it in the form of the

Gohonzon, the object of devotion, thereby establishing a means by which all people can reveal their innate Buddhahood.

This chapter introduces the basics of the doctrine of the Ten Worlds—the principle that is the key to inner transformation—as well as the significance of the Gohonzon.

President Ikeda discusses the core teaching of Nichiren Buddhism that, through chanting Nam-myoho-renge-kyo with faith in the Gohonzon, we can establish the world of Buddhahood as the foundation of our lives and turn all suffering into nourishment for developing a higher state of life. Further, we can transform not only our own lives but help others do the same, and contribute to the betterment and prosperity of society.

Three Thousand Realms in a Single Moment of Life

The essence of the teachings of Shakyamuni Buddha in India culminates in the Lotus Sutra, which reveals the principle that all living beings can attain Buddhahood.

Based on the Lotus Sutra, the Great Teacher T'ien-t'ai (538–97), founder of the T'ien-t'ai school of Buddhism in China, systematized the totality of life in his doctrine of three thousand realms in a single moment of life. "A single moment of life" refers to life at each moment. The "three thousand realms" represents the integration of four concepts that focus on differing aspects of life—the Ten Worlds, their mutual possession, the ten factors of life, and the three realms of existence (10 x 10 x 10 x 3 = 3,000).

The Ten Worlds are the ten states of life: hell, hunger, animality, anger, humanity, heaven, learning, realization, bodhisattva, and Buddhahood. They are also referred to as the realms of hell, hungry spirits, animals, *asuras,* human beings, heavenly beings, voice-hearers, cause-awakened ones, bodhisattvas, and Buddhas.

The mutual possession of the Ten Worlds means that each of the Ten Worlds has all of the Ten Worlds inherent within it.

The ten factors of life are ten aspects shared by all living beings of the Ten Worlds—appearance, nature, entity, power, influence, internal cause, relation, latent effect, manifest effect, and their consistency from beginning to end.

The three realms of existence are the realm of the five components (form, perception, conception, volition, and consciousness, which are said to merge to form an individual being); the realm of living beings; and the realm of the environment. This concept explains the existence and sphere of activity of beings of the Ten Worlds.

The principle of three thousand realms in a single moment of life reveals the nature of life and the universe in their entirety—that all phenomena and all forces of the universe exist in every single moment of life.

Based on the Lotus Sutra and T'ien-t'ai's principle of three thousand realms in a single moment of life, Nichiren Daishonin expressed in the form of the Gohonzon (object of devotion) of Nam-myoho-renge-kyo the ultimate truth of life and the universe to which he became enlightened.

And he established a practice-oriented Buddhist teaching that enables all people to fundamentally transform their lives.

The practice of Nichiren Buddhism empowers us to transform not only our own lives but also to make a positive difference to the lives of those around us, our environment, and all humankind. Because the teaching of Nichiren Buddhism is not empty theory but, rather, thoroughly directed toward the actual transformation of our lives and the world, it is known as the Buddhism of the "actual three thousand realms in a single moment of life."

—The Editors

2.1 Heaven and Hell Exist Within Our Own Lives

The way we perceive the world around us is largely influenced by our state of life. In this excerpt, President Ikeda explains that Nichiren Buddhism is a powerful teaching that enables us to elevate our state of life, improve our environment, and actualize genuinely happy lives for ourselves and prosperity for society as a whole, while positively transforming the land in which we live.

■ The English poet John Milton (1608–74) wrote, "The mind is its own place, and in it self / Can make a Heav'n of Hell, a Hell of Heav'n."[5] This statement, a product of the poet's profound insight, resonates with the Buddhist teaching of three thousand realms in a single moment of life.

How we see the world and feel about our lives is determined

solely by our inner life condition. Nichiren writes: "Hungry spirits perceive the Ganges River as fire, human beings perceive it as water, and heavenly beings perceive it as amrita.[6] Though the water is the same, it appears differently according to one's karmic reward from the past" (WND-1, 486).

"Karmic reward from the past" refers to our present life state, which is the result of past actions or causes created through our own words, thoughts, and deeds. That state of life determines our view of and feelings toward the external world.

The same circumstances may be perceived as utter bliss by one person and unbearable misfortune by another. And while some people may love the place where they live, thinking it's the best place ever, others may hate it and constantly seek to find happiness somewhere else.

Nichiren Buddhism is a teaching that enables us to elevate our inner state of life, realizing genuinely happy lives for ourselves as well as prosperity for society. It is the great teaching of the "actual three thousand realms in a single moment of life," making it possible for us to transform the place where we dwell into the Land of Eternally Tranquil Light.[7]

Moreover, the good fortune, benefit, and joy we gain through living in accord with the eternal Law [of Nam-myoho-renge-kyo] are not temporary. In the same way that trees steadily add growth rings with each passing year, our lives accumulate good fortune that will endure throughout the three existences of past, present, and future. In contrast, worldly wealth and fame as well as various amusements and pleasures—no matter how glamorous or exciting they may seem for a time—are fleeting and insubstantial.

From a speech at the 1st Wakayama Prefecture General Meeting, Kansai Training Center, Wakayama Prefecture, Japan, March 24, 1988.

2.2 Buddhahood Is the Sun Within Us

In this excerpt, President Ikeda gives a brief overview of the Ten Worlds and their mutual possession—concepts that lie at the heart of the Buddhist philosophy of life. He also underscores how Nichiren, through his teaching, established a practice based on faith in the Gohonzon as the means for all people to manifest the highest and noblest state of life, that of Buddhahood.

■ Life, which is constantly changing from moment to moment, can be broadly categorized into ten states, which Buddhism articulates as the Ten Worlds. These consist of the six paths—the worlds of hell, hunger, animality, anger, humanity, and heaven—and the four noble worlds—the worlds of learning, realization, bodhisattva, and Buddhahood. The true reality of life is that it always possesses all ten of these potential states.

None of the Ten Worlds that appear in our lives at any given moment remain fixed or constant. They change instant by instant. Buddhism's deep insight into this dynamic nature of life is expressed as the principle of the mutual possession of the Ten Worlds.

In his treatise "The Object of Devotion for Observing the Mind," Nichiren illustrates clearly and simply how the world of humanity contains within it the other nine worlds:

> When we look from time to time at a person's face, we find him or her sometimes joyful, sometimes enraged, and sometimes calm. At times greed appears in the person's face, at times foolishness, and at times perversity. Rage is the world of hell, greed is that of hungry spirits, foolishness is that of

> animals, perversity is that of asuras, joy is that of heaven [heavenly beings], and calmness is that of human beings. (WND-1, 358)

The nine worlds are continually emerging and becoming dormant within us. This is something that we can see, sense, and recognize in our own daily lives.

It is important to note here that the teachings of Buddhism from the very beginning were always concerned with enabling people to manifest the noble and infinitely powerful life state of Buddhahood. And, indeed, that should always be the purpose of Buddhist practice. Focusing on this point, the great teaching of Nichiren Daishonin, by establishing the correct object of devotion [the Gohonzon of Nam-myoho-renge-kyo], sets forth a practical means for revealing our inner Buddhahood. As such, Nichiren Buddhism is a practice open to all people.

A look at history to this day shows that humanity is still trapped in the cycle of the six paths, or lower six worlds. The character for "earth" (*ji*) is contained in the Japanese word for "hell" (*jigoku;* literally "earth prison"), imparting the meaning of being bound or shackled to something of the lowest or basest level. Humanity and society can never achieve substantial revitalization unless people give serious thought to casting off the shackles of these lower worlds and elevating their state of life. Even in the midst of this troubled and corrupt world, Buddhism discovers in human life the highest and most dignified potential of Buddhahood.

Though our lives may constantly move through the six paths, we can activate the limitless life force of Buddhahood by focusing our minds on the correct object of devotion and achieving the "fusion of reality and wisdom."[8]

Buddhahood is difficult to describe in words. Unlike the other nine worlds, it has no concrete expression. It is the ultimate function of life that moves the nine worlds in the direction of boundless value.

Even on cloudy or rainy days, by the time a plane reaches an altitude of about 30,000 feet, it is flying high above the clouds amid bright sunshine and can proceed smoothly on its course. In the same way, no matter how painful or difficult our daily existence may be, if we make the sun in our hearts shine brightly, we can overcome all adversity with calm composure. That inner sun is the life state of Buddhahood.

In one sense, as the Daishonin states in *The Record of the Orally Transmitted Teachings*, "'Bodhisattva' is a preliminary step toward the attainment of the effect of Buddhahood" (OTT, 87). The world of bodhisattva is characterized by taking action for the sake of the Law, people, and society. Without such bodhisattva practice as our foundation, we cannot attain Buddhahood. Buddhahood is not something realized simply through conceptual understanding. Even reading countless Buddhist scriptures or books on Buddhism will not lead one to true enlightenment.

In addition, attaining Buddhahood doesn't mean that we become someone different. We remain who we are, living out our lives in the reality of society, where the nine worlds—especially the six paths—prevail. A genuine Buddhist philosophy does not present enlightenment or Buddhas as something mysterious or otherworldly.

What is important for us as human beings is to elevate our lives from a lower to a higher state, to expand our lives from a closed, narrow state of life to one that is infinitely vast and encompassing. Buddhahood represents the supreme state of life.

Adapted from the dialogue On Life and Buddhism, *published in Japanese in November 1986.*

2.3 Establishing the World of Buddhahood as Our Basic Life Tendency

Based on the principle of the mutual possession of the Ten Worlds, President Ikeda in this excerpt introduces the idea that each of us has a basic or habitual life tendency—a tendency that has been formed through our repeated past actions encompassing speech, thought, and deed. He further clarifies that "attaining Buddhahood" means establishing the world of Buddhahood as this basic life tendency.

Yet even with Buddhahood as our basic life tendency, we will still face the sufferings of the nine worlds that are the reality of our existence. Irrespective of the problems and hardships we may encounter in life, however, compassion, hope, and joy arising from the world of Buddhahood will well forth within us.

In his treatise "The Object of Devotion for Observing the Mind," Nichiren offers an example of "the nine worlds inherent in Buddhahood" (WND-1, 357), citing the Lotus Sutra passage where Shakyamuni states: "Thus since I attained Buddhahood, an extremely long period of time has passed. . . . I have constantly abided here without ever entering extinction. . . . Originally I practiced the bodhisattva way, and the life span that I acquired then has yet to come to an end" (LSOC, 267–68). We could say that a practical expression of this passage can be found in living our lives with Buddhahood as our basic life tendency.

■ One way to view the principle that each of us is an entity of the mutual possession of the Ten Worlds is to look at it from the perspective of our basic life tendency. While we all possess the Ten Worlds, our lives often lean toward one particular life state more than others—for instance, some people's lives are basically inclined toward the world of hell, while others tend naturally toward the world of bodhisattva. This could be called the "habit pattern" of one's life, a predisposition formed through karmic causes that a person has accumulated from the past.

Just as a spring returns to its original shape after being stretched, people tend to revert to their own basic tendency. But even if one's basic life tendency is the world of hell, it doesn't mean that one will remain in that state twenty-four hours a day. That person will still move from one life state to another—for instance, sometimes manifesting the world of humanity, sometimes the world of anger, and so on. Likewise, those whose basic life tendency is the world of anger—driven by the desire to always be better than others—will also sometimes manifest higher worlds such as heaven or bodhisattva. Even if they momentarily manifest the world of bodhisattva, however, they will quickly revert to their basic life tendency of the world of anger.

Changing our basic life tendency means carrying out our human revolution and fundamentally transforming our state of life. It means changing our mind-set or resolve on the deepest level. The kind of life we live is decided by our basic life tendency. For example, those whose basic life tendency is the world of hunger are as though on board a ship called *hunger*. While sailing ahead in the world of hunger, they will sometimes experience joy and sometimes suffering. Though there are various ups and downs, the ship unerringly proceeds on its set course. Consequently, for those on board this ship, everything they see will be colored in the hues of the world of hunger. And even after they die, their lives will merge with the world of hunger inherent in the universe.

Establishing the world of Buddhahood as our basic life tendency is what it means to "attain Buddhahood." Of course, even with the world of Buddhahood as our basic life tendency, we won't be free of problems or suffering, because we will still possess the other nine worlds. But the foundation of our lives will become one of hope, and we will increasingly experience a condition of security and joy.

My mentor, Josei Toda, once explained this as follows:

> Even if you fall ill, simply have the attitude, "I'm all right. I know that if I chant to the Gohonzon, I will get well." Isn't the world of Buddhahood a state of life in which we can live with total peace of mind? That said, however, given that the nine worlds are inherent in the world of Buddhahood, we might still occasionally become angry or have to deal with problems. Therefore, enjoying total peace of mind doesn't mean that we have to renounce anger or some such thing. When something worrisome happens, it's only natural to be worried. But in the innermost depths of our lives, we will have a profound sense of security. This is what it means to be a Buddha. . . .
>
> If we can regard life itself as an absolute joy, isn't that being a Buddha? Doesn't that mean attaining the same life state as the Daishonin? Even when faced with the threat of being beheaded, the Daishonin remained calm and composed. If it had been us in that situation, we'd have been in a state of complete panic! When the Daishonin was exiled to the hostile environment of Sado Island, he continued instructing his disciples on various matters and produced such important writings as "The Opening of the Eyes" and "The Object of Devotion for Observing the Mind." If he didn't have unshakable peace of mind, he would never have been able to compose such great treatises [under such difficult circumstances].[9]

Our daily practice of gongyo—reciting portions of the Lotus Sutra and chanting Nam-myoho-renge-kyo—is a solemn ceremony in which our lives become one with the life of the Buddha.

By applying ourselves steadfastly and persistently to this practice for manifesting our inherent Buddhahood, we firmly establish the world of Buddhahood in our lives so that it is solid and unshakable like the earth. On this foundation, this solid stage, we can freely enact at each moment the drama of the nine worlds.

Moreover, kosen-rufu is the challenge to transform the fundamental life state of society into that of Buddhahood. The key to this lies in increasing the number of those who share our noble aspirations.

When we base ourselves on faith in Nichiren Buddhism, absolutely no effort we make is ever wasted.

When we establish Buddhahood as our basic life tendency, we can move toward a future of hope while creating positive value from all our activities in the nine worlds, both past and present. In fact, all of our hardships and struggles in the nine worlds become the nourishment that strengthens the world of Buddhahood in our lives.

In accord with the Buddhist principle that "earthly desires lead to enlightenment," sufferings (earthly desires, or the deluded impulses of the nine worlds) all become the "firewood" or fuel for gaining happiness (enlightenment, or the world of Buddhahood). This is similar to how our bodies digest food and turn it into energy.

A Buddha who has no connection to the actual sufferings of the nine worlds is not a genuine Buddha—namely, one who embodies the mutual possession of the Ten Worlds. This is the essential message of "Life Span," the sixteenth chapter of the Lotus Sutra.

The world of Buddhahood can also be described as a state of life where one willingly takes on even hellish suffering. This is the world of hell contained in the world of Buddhahood. It is characterized by empathy and hardships deliberately taken on for the happiness and welfare of others, and it arises from a sense of responsibility and compassion. Courageously taking on problems and sufferings for the sake of others strengthens the world of Buddhahood in our lives.

Adapted from the dialogue The Wisdom of the Lotus Sutra,
published in Japanese in December 1998.

2.4 The Gohonzon Encompasses All of the Ten Worlds

The Gohonzon inscribed by Nichiren Daishonin has Nam-myoho-renge-kyo—the ultimate Law of the universe and life—in the center, surrounded by representative beings of the Ten Worlds. In this excerpt, President Ikeda explains how, through our practice of reciting the sutra and chanting Nam-myoho-renge-kyo to the Gohonzon, the Ten Worlds within us, just as depicted on the Gohonzon, come to be based on the Mystic Law and function to create positive value and contribute to our happiness and attainment of Buddhahood.

■ The Japanese word *honzon* means "object of fundamental respect or devotion"—in other words, the object that we respect and devote ourselves to as the basis of our lives. It is only natural, therefore, that what we take as our object of devotion will have a decisive impact on the direction of our lives.

Traditionally, objects of devotion in Buddhism were often statues of the Buddha. In some cases, paintings of the Buddha were used. While statues of the Buddha did not exist in early Buddhism, they later began to appear in the Gandhara region of northwest India, due to the influence of Grecian culture. They were, if you like, a product of cultural exchange on the ancient Silk Road. Through statues and paintings, people became familiar with the image of the Buddha, leading them to arouse faith in the Buddha and revere him.

The object of devotion in Nichiren Buddhism, however, is the Gohonzon,[10] which consists of written characters. In that sense, rather than simply a visual or graphic depiction, I would call it the highest and noblest expression of the world of the intellect, of the great wisdom of the Buddha of the Latter Day of the Law. In this respect alone, Nichiren's object of devotion is fundamentally different from those traditionally worshipped in Buddhism.

Written words are wondrous; they have tremendous power. Take people's names, for example. When people sign their names, it embodies everything about them—their character, social position, power, emotional and physical condition, personal history, and karma.

Similarly, Nam-myoho-renge-kyo [which is inscribed down the center of the Gohonzon] encompasses all things in the universe. All phenomena are expressions of the Mystic Law, as the Great Teacher T'ien-t'ai indicates when he states (in *Great Concentration and Insight*), "Arising is the arising of the essential nature of the Law [Dharma nature], and extinction is the extinction of that nature" (WND-1, 216).

The true aspect of the ever-changing universe (all phenomena) is perfectly expressed, just as it is, in the Gohonzon. The true aspect of the macrocosm of the universe is exactly the same for the microcosm of each of our lives. This is what Nichiren tells us in his writings. In addition, the Gohonzon embodies the principle of the "oneness of the Person and the Law" and expresses the enlightened life state of Nichiren Daishonin, the Buddha of the Latter Day of the Law.

In that sense, the Gohonzon inscribed by the Daishonin is an embodiment of the fundamental Law of the universe that should be revered by all people; it is the true object of fundamental devotion.

The universe contains both positive and negative workings or functions. Representatives of the Ten Worlds are all depicted on the Gohonzon—from the Buddhas Shakyamuni and Many Treasures, who represent the world of Buddhahood, to Devadatta, who represents the world of hell. Nichiren teaches that such representatives of the positive and negative workings of the universe are all without exception illuminated by the light of Nam-myoho-renge-kyo, enabling them to display "the dignified attributes that they inherently possess," and that this is the function of the Gohonzon (see WND-1, 832).

When we recite the sutra and chant Nam-myoho-renge-kyo to the Gohonzon, both the positive and negative tendencies in our lives begin to manifest "the dignified attributes that they inherently possess." The world of hell with its painful suffering, the world of hunger with its insatiable cravings, the world of anger with its perverse rage—all come to function to contribute to our happiness and to the creation of value. When we base our lives on the Mystic Law, the life states that drag us toward suffering and unhappiness move in the opposite, positive direction. It is as if sufferings become the "firewood" that fuels the flames of joy, wisdom, and compassion. The Mystic Law and faith are what ignite those flames.

In addition, when we chant Nam-myoho-renge-kyo, the positive forces of the universe—represented by all Buddhas, bodhisattvas, and heavenly deities such as Brahma and Shakra (the tutelary gods of Buddhism)—will shine even more brightly, their power and influence increasing and expanding endlessly. The gods of the sun and moon that exist in the microcosm of our lives will also shine brilliantly to illuminate the darkness within. All of the workings—both positive and negative—of the Ten Worlds and the three thousand realms function together at full power, propelling us toward a life of happiness, a life imbued with the four virtues of eternity, happiness, true self, and purity.

In life, it is only natural that we sometimes fall ill. Based on the teaching of the Mystic Law, however, we can look at illness as an inherent part of life. Seeing it this way, we will not be swayed by illness when it happens to us, or allow it to be a source of suffering and distress. Viewed from the perspective of the eternity of life, we are definitely on the way to establishing a "greater self" overflowing with absolute happiness. In addition, we will be able to overcome any obstacle we encounter in life, using it as a springboard for developing a new, more expansive state of being. Life will be enjoyable and death will be peaceful, marking the solemn departure for our next wonderful lifetime.

When winter arrives, trees are, for a while, bare of flowers and leaves. But they possess the life force to grow fresh green leaves when spring comes. Similar to this, but on an even more profound level, for us, as practitioners of the Mystic Law, death is the dynamic process by which our life itself transitions, without pain, to quickly begin its next mission-filled existence.

From a speech delivered at an SGI-USA Youth Training Session, Malibu Training Center, California, February 20, 1990.

2.5 "Never Seek This Gohonzon Outside Yourself"

Sometimes people think that the Gohonzon is greater than themselves. In this excerpt, however, President Ikeda discusses the profound significance of Nichiren's teaching that the Gohonzon exists within our own lives. We possess within us boundless life force and infinite wisdom, which our practice of Nichiren Buddhism enables us to tap freely.

■ In any religion, the object of worship or devotion holds a place of prime importance. What, then, is the true meaning of the object of devotion, or the Gohonzon, in Nichiren Buddhism?

In "The Real Aspect of the Gohonzon," the Daishonin states: "Never seek this Gohonzon outside yourself. The Gohonzon exists only within the mortal flesh of us ordinary people who embrace the Lotus Sutra and chant Nam-myoho-renge-kyo" (WND-1, 832). Discussing this passage in one of his lectures, Mr. Toda said:

> Although we may pray to this great Gohonzon thinking it exists outside us, the reality is that it resides directly within the lives of us who chant Nam-myoho-renge-kyo with faith in the Gohonzon of the Three Great Secret Laws. This passage from the Daishonin is truly inspiring.
>
> Those who do not yet have faith in the Mystic Law are people at the "stage of being a Buddha in theory" [the first of the six stages of practice],[11] where the Buddha nature, while appearing vaguely to be present, does not function in the least. We [Soka Gakkai members], on the other hand, because we chant to the Gohonzon, are at the "stage of hearing the name and words of the truth" [the second of the six stages of practice]. At this stage, the Gohonzon already shines brilliantly within us.
>
> The degree to which it shines will differ, however, depending upon the strength of each person's faith. It's like a light bulb. A high-wattage light bulb shines brightly, and a low-wattage light bulb shines faintly.
>
> To continue with the analogy of a light bulb, for those who haven't yet embraced the Mystic Law, the light bulb isn't connected to a power source. Whereas for us, practitioners of the Mystic Law, the light bulb that is the Gohonzon is turned on. Therefore, our lives shine brightly.[12]

Everything depends on the strength of our faith. When we have strong faith, our life itself becomes a "cluster of blessings" (WND-1, 832), which is how the Daishonin describes the Gohonzon. He further states, "This Gohonzon also is found only in the two characters for faith"[13] (WND-1, 832).

People of strong faith, therefore, never reach a deadlock. No matter what happens, they can transform everything into a source of benefit and happiness. Naturally, in the long course of our lives, we are bound to encounter various kinds of problems and suffering. But we can turn all difficulties into nourishment for developing a higher state of life. In this respect, for practitioners of Nichiren Buddhism, everything is ultimately a source of benefit and happiness at the most profound level. The word "unhappiness" does not exist in the vocabulary of those who have strong faith.

Toward the end of his *Commentary on "The Object of Devotion for Observing the Mind,"* Nichikan (1665–1726), a great restorer of Nichiren Buddhism who began the task of systematizing Nichiren's teachings, writes:

> When we embrace faith in this object of devotion [the Gohonzon] and chant Nam-myoho-renge-kyo, our lives immediately become the object of devotion of three thousand realms in a single moment of life; they become the life of Nichiren Daishonin. This is the true meaning of the phrase "he [the Buddha] then adorned the necks of the ignorant people of the latter age [with the five characters of Myoho-renge-kyo]"[14] (see WND-1, 376). Therefore, we must venerate the power of the Buddha and the power of the Law and strive to develop our own power of faith and power of practice. We must not spend our lives in vain and regret it for all eternity, as the Daishonin says (see WND-1, 622).[15]

In this passage, Nichikan clearly states that, through faith in the Gohonzon, our lives can instantly manifest the object of devotion and life state of Nichiren Daishonin. It was for this very purpose that the Daishonin inscribed the Gohonzon. Here, we find the supreme essence of Nichiren Buddhism.

Faith enables us to manifest the Gohonzon that exists within us; it allows us to bring forth the diamond-like state of the Buddha and make it shine brightly.

Within the depths of our lives, we each inherently possess boundless life force and a wellspring of infinite wisdom. Faith allows us to freely tap that inner life force and wisdom.

Mr. Toda often used to say: "What's inside you comes out. What's not there, won't." The strong and pure state of Buddhahood and the weak and base states of hell, hunger, and animality all exist within our lives and are manifested in response to causes and conditions in our environment.

Since life is eternal throughout the three existences of past, present, and future, our past karma may also assail us in the present in the form of some major problem or suffering. But just as the cause of suffering lies within our lives, we also possess the power to transform our suffering into happiness. This is the power of the life state of Buddhahood.

As Mr. Toda declared, ultimately human beings are the product of what lies inside them, no more, no less.

It's vital, therefore, that we each cultivate the "earth" of our lives and put down deep and extensive "roots" of happiness. We must manifest the Gohonzon that exists within us and forge a self that is as unshakable as a mighty tree. In terms of our life state, this will be expressed as outstanding humanity and exemplary behavior, while in terms of our daily lives, it will manifest as benefit and good fortune.

The crucial point is whether we have faith. We must never make light of the Daishonin's assertion that "It is the heart that is important" (WND-1, 1000).

What matters is not form or a person's position or wealth. Those who have faith in their hearts are truly happy.

From a speech at a Representatives Gathering Commemorating April 2, the anniversary of second Soka Gakkai President Josei Toda's passing, held at the Ota Culture Center, Tokyo, April 3, 1993.

2.6 The Gohonzon Is the "Mirror" That Reflects Our Lives

In this excerpt, President Ikeda explains that the Gohonzon is like a mirror that reflects the true nature of our own lives. The Gohonzon is the ultimate expression of Buddha wisdom, enabling all people to attain enlightenment by perceiving the true reality of their lives.

■ I would like to speak about an important point with regard to our attitude in faith through the analogy of mirrors. In Buddhism, mirrors have a wide variety of meanings and are often used to explain and illustrate various doctrines. Here, I would like to briefly discuss an example related to our Buddhist practice.

Nichiren Daishonin writes:

> A bronze mirror will reflect the form of a person but it will not reflect that person's mind. The Lotus Sutra, however, reveals not only the person's form but that person's mind as well. And it reveals not only the mind; it reflects, without the least concealment, that person's past actions and future as well. (WND-2, 619)

Mirrors reflect our face and outward form. The mirror of Buddhism, however, reveals the intangible aspect of our lives. Mirrors, which function by virtue of the laws of light and reflection, are a product of human ingenuity. On the other hand, the Gohonzon, based on the Law of the universe and life, is the ultimate expression of Buddha wisdom. It enables us to attain Buddhahood by providing us with a means to perceive the true reality of our lives. Just as a mirror is indispensable for grooming our face and hair, we need a mirror of life that allows us to look closely at ourselves and our lives if we are to lead a happier and more beautiful existence.

Incidentally, as indicated in the Daishonin's reference to a bronze mirror in the quote I just mentioned, mirrors in ancient times were made of polished metal, including copper, bronze, and other alloys. Tin was also often mixed in. Unlike today's mirrors made of glass, these ancient mirrors could only produce somewhat blurred reflections. Bronze mirrors not only reflected poorly but also tarnished very quickly. Therefore, unless they were polished regularly, they became unusable. Polishing these mirrors required special skill and was carried out by trained craftsmen called "mirror polishers." These bronze mirrors were commonly used during the Daishonin's day.

This tradition of mirror polishing also underlies the following famous passage from "On Attaining Buddhahood in This Lifetime":

> A tarnished mirror . . . will shine like a jewel when polished. A mind now clouded by the illusions of the innate darkness of life is like a tarnished mirror, but when polished, it is sure to become like a clear mirror, reflecting the essential nature of phenomena [Dharma nature] and the true aspect of reality. (WND-1, 4)

Originally, every person's life is a brilliantly shining mirror. Differences arise depending on whether one polishes this mirror.

A polished mirror corresponds to the life state of the Buddha, whereas a tarnished mirror corresponds to that of an ordinary unenlightened being. Chanting Nam-myoho-renge-kyo is how we polish our lives. Not only do we undertake this practice ourselves, we also endeavor to teach others about the Mystic Law so that they can make the mirror of their lives shine brightly too. In this respect, we could be called master "mirror polishers" in the realm of life. Even though people work hard at polishing their appearance, they often tend to neglect polishing their lives. While they fret over blemishes on their face, they remain unconcerned about blemishes in the depths of their lives!

In the famous novel *The Picture of Dorian Gray* by Oscar Wilde (1854–1900), the youthful protagonist, Dorian Gray, is so handsome that he is called a "young Adonis." An artist who wishes to immortalize Dorian's beauty paints his portrait. It is a brilliant work, an embodiment of Dorian's youthfulness and beauty. It is then that something mysterious begins to happen. Dorian's beauty does not fade, even as he is gradually tempted by a friend into a life of hedonism and immorality. Although the years go by, he remains as youthful and radiant as ever. Strangely, however, the portrait begins to turn ugly and lusterless, reflecting Dorian's dissolute life.

Then, one day, Dorian cruelly breaks a young woman's heart, driving her to commit suicide. At that time, the face in the portrait takes on an evil and savage expression that is frightening to behold. As Dorian's disreputable behavior continues, so does the hideous transformation of the portrait. Dorian is filled with horror. This picture would forever portray the face of his soul in all its ugliness. Even if he were to die, it would continue to eloquently convey the truth.

Though Dorian makes a token effort to be a better person, the picture does not change. He decides to destroy the portrait, thinking that if it were gone, he could break free from his past. So he plunges a knife into the painting. At that moment, hearing screams, his neighbors rush over to find a portrait of the handsome, young Dorian and, collapsed before it, an aged, repulsive-looking man, Dorian, with a knife sticking in his chest.

The painting had been a portrait of Dorian's soul, his inner face, into which the effects of his actions had been etched without the slightest omission.

Though we can cover imperfections on our face with cosmetics, we cannot conceal imperfections on the inner face of our lives. The law of cause and effect is strict and inexorable.

Buddhism teaches that unseen virtue brings about visible reward. In the world of Buddhism, everything counts. Being two-faced or pretentious, therefore, serves us absolutely no purpose.

Our inner face that is engraved with the positive and negative causes we make is to an extent reflected in our appearance. There is also a saying "The face is the mirror of the mind."

Just as we look into a mirror when we groom our face, we need a mirror that reflects the depths of our life to beautifully polish our inner face. This mirror is none other than the Gohonzon for "observing the mind."

In "The Object of Devotion for Observing the Mind," Nichiren explains the meaning of "observing the mind," saying: "Only when we look into a clear mirror do we see, for the first time, that we are endowed with all six sense organs [eyes, ears, nose, tongue, body, and mind]"[16] (WND-1, 356).

Similarly, "observing the mind" means to perceive that one's mind, or life, contains the Ten Worlds, and in particular, the world of Buddhahood. It was to enable people to do this that Nichiren bestowed the Gohonzon for "observing the mind" upon all humankind.

In his *Commentary on "The Object of Devotion for Observing the Mind,"* Nichikan likens the Gohonzon to a mirror, stating, "The true object of devotion can be compared to a clear mirror."[17] And in *The Record of the Orally Transmitted Teachings,* Nichiren says, "The five characters Myoho-renge-kyo [embodied in the Gohonzon] similarly reflect the ten thousand phenomena [i.e., all phenomena],[18] not overlooking a single one of them" (OTT, 51). The Gohonzon is the clearest of all mirrors, reflecting the entire universe exactly as it is. When we chant to the Gohonzon, we can perceive the true nature of our lives and manifest the world of Buddhahood.

Our attitude or determination in faith is perfectly reflected in the mirror of the Gohonzon and mirrored in the universe. This accords with the principle of three thousand realms in a single moment of life.

In a letter to Abutsu-bo, one of his loyal disciples on Sado Island, the Daishonin writes: "You may think you offered gifts to the treasure tower of the Thus Come One Many Treasures, but that is not so. You offered them to yourself" (WND-1, 299).

An attitude in faith that reveres and honors the Gohonzon dignifies and honors the treasure tower of our own lives. When we chant to the Gohonzon, all Buddhas and bodhisattvas throughout the universe will instantly lend their support and protection. On the other hand, if we slander the Gohonzon, the opposite will be true [i.e., such support and protection will not be forthcoming].

Accordingly, our attitude or mind is extremely important. Our deep-seated attitude or determination in faith has a subtle and far-reaching influence.

There may be times, for instance, when you feel reluctant to do gongyo or take part in SGI activities. That state of mind will be unerringly reflected in the universe, as if on the surface of a clear mirror. The heavenly deities will then also feel reluctant to play their part, and they will naturally fail to exert their full protective powers.

On the other hand, when you joyfully do gongyo and carry out activities for kosen-rufu with the determination to accumulate even more good fortune in your life, the heavenly deities will be delighted and actively function to support you. If you are going to take some action anyway, it is to your advantage to do so willingly and joyfully.

If you carry out your Buddhist practice reluctantly with a sense that it's a waste of time, doubt and complaint will erase your benefits. Of course, if you continue in this way, you will fail to perceive any benefit from your practice, only further reconfirming your incorrect conviction that there's no point in practicing. This is a vicious circle.

If you practice Nichiren Buddhism filled with doubt and skepticism, you will get results that are, at best, vague and unsatisfactory. This is the reflection of your own weak conviction in faith on the mirror of the universe. On the other hand, when you stand up with strong conviction in faith, you will accrue limitless good fortune and benefit.

It's important that we vibrantly open up our mind of faith, which is both extremely subtle and far-reaching, while striving for self-mastery. When we do so, both our life and state of mind will expand limitlessly, and every action we take will become a source of benefit. Deeply mastering the subtle and far-reaching workings of the mind is the key to faith and to attaining Buddhahood in this lifetime.

There is a Russian proverb that says, "Don't blame the mirror if your face is awry." The reflection in the mirror is our own. But some people get angry at the mirror!

In the same way, our happiness or unhappiness is entirely a reflection of the positive and negative causes accumulated in our lives. We cannot blame others for our misfortunes. This is even more so in the realm of faith.

There is a Japanese folk tale about a small village where no one had a mirror. In those days, mirrors were priceless. A man, returning from a trip to the capital, handed his wife a mirror as a souvenir. It was the first time for her to see one. Looking into the mirror, she exclaimed: "Who on earth is this woman? You must've brought a girl back with you from the capital!" And so a big fight ensued.

Though this is an amusing anecdote, many people become angry or distraught over phenomena that are actually nothing but a reflection of their own lives—their state of mind and the causes that they have created. Like the wife in the story who exclaims "Who on earth is this woman?" they do not realize their own folly.

Ignorant of the mirror of life of Buddhism, such people cannot see themselves as they really are. And ignorant of their own true self, they naturally cannot give proper guidance and direction to others, nor can they discern the true nature of occurrences in society.

From a speech at an SGI-USA Women's Meeting, Soka University Los Angeles Campus, Calabasas, California, February 27, 1990.

CHAPTER 3

The Practice for Transforming Our State of Life

Introduction

In the previous chapter, we examined the principle for transforming our lives taught in Nichiren Buddhism. In this chapter, we explore the most fundamental practice for carrying out that transformation, the practice known as gongyo.[19]

Gongyo in Nichiren Buddhism consists of reciting portions of the "Expedient Means" and "The Life Span of the Thus Come One," the second and sixteenth chapters of the Lotus Sutra, and chanting daimoku, or Nam-myoho-renge-kyo, with faith in the Gohonzon.

The Lotus Sutra is the Buddha's highest teaching, the quintessence of Buddhist wisdom and compassion. Nichiren Daishonin identified the essential teaching or Law implicit in the text of the Lotus Sutra as Nam-myoho-renge-kyo and embodied it in the form of the Gohonzon, the object of devotion for our faith and practice.

SGI President Ikeda explains, based on the principle of the "actual three thousand realms in a single moment of life" taught by Nichiren, that Nam-myoho-renge-kyo is the fundamental Law that pervades life and the universe. He describes gongyo as a ceremony in which our lives commune with the universe. When we chant Nam-myoho-renge-kyo with faith in the Gohonzon, we align our individual lives with the rhythm of the Mystic Law of the universe and can tap unlimited wisdom, compassion, and courage.

As Nichiren Daishonin indicates in various writings, gongyo encapsulates within it the significance of all Buddhist practices. Even without having a deep understanding of Buddhist doctrines or engaging in austere practices that are not feasible for most, we can elevate our life state infinitely by basing ourselves on the practice of gongyo. In this way, Nichiren Buddhism is a teaching for and accessible to all people.

President Ikeda further stresses that, in seeking to genuinely transform our lives, it is essential that we not only exert ourselves in the practice of gongyo but also take courageous action to effect positive change.

3.1 Gongyo: A Ceremony in Which Our Lives Commune With the Universe

In this excerpt, President Ikeda clarifies that Nam-myoho-renge-kyo is the fundamental Law pervading all life and the universe. He bases his discussion on the Buddhist concept of the interconnectedness of our lives and the universe. Various Buddhist texts highlight this principle, such as Miao-lo's Annotations on "Great Concentration and Insight," *which states: "One understands that everything that is contained within this body of ours is modeled after heaven and earth"*[20] *(WND-2, 848). Through the practice of chanting Nam-myoho-renge-kyo, President Ikeda goes on to say, we can bring forth in our lives the limitless power of the Mystic Law.*

■ Gongyo—reciting portions of the Lotus Sutra and chanting Nam-myoho-renge-kyo— is a ceremony in which our lives commune with the universe. It is an act through which, based on the Gohonzon, we can vibrantly draw forth the life force of the universe within the cosmos of our lives. We exist. We have life. The universe, too, is a giant living entity. Life is the universe and the universe is life. Each of us is a living entity, just like the universe. We are our own miniature universe.

One scholar, observing that the human body is made of the same elements produced by stars, has called human beings "children of the stars." Our bodies are a microcosm of the universe. Not only are they made of the same matter as the universe, but they also follow the same process of generation and disintegration, the same rhythm of life and death, that pervades the cosmos. All physical laws—such as gravity and the conservation of energy—also affect and operate in the microcosm of each living entity.

The earth takes 365 days, five hours and forty-eight minutes to complete one revolution around the sun. It, too, operates according to a rigorous order. The human body, meanwhile, is said to have more than 60 trillion individual cells. When they function each day in a well-ordered fashion, correctly carrying out their respective jobs, we enjoy good health. The complexity and precision of the human body are truly wondrous. Likewise, if the earth were to veer even slightly from its present orbit around the sun, we would be in serious trouble. Everything hangs in a delicate balance, governed by the strict principle that life and the universe are one. The same is true of each individual life—of each microcosm.

Science has directed its attention to the investigation of real, yet invisible, natural laws. Such investigation has led to the invention of many machines and devices that apply those laws. An understanding of the principles of buoyancy, for instance, led to the development of seagoing vessels. Likewise, the discovery of the laws of aerodynamics led to the invention of aircraft, and insight into the workings of electromagnetic waves paved the way for the development of radio and television. These natural laws, however, are only partial laws of the universe.

Buddhism, on the other hand, developed out of the search for and discovery of the ultimate Law of life that is the source and foundation of all other laws and principles. This ultimate Law of life is the Mystic Law.

The Mystic Law is also invisible, yet it, too, exists without a doubt. Nichiren Daishonin inscribed the Gohonzon so that we could bring forth the power of the Mystic Law from within our own lives. That is why second Soka Gakkai President Josei Toda said, "I apologize for using such a simplistic analogy, but the Gohonzon can be likened to a happiness-producing device."

When we do gongyo the microcosm of our individual lives harmonizes seamlessly with the macrocosm of the universe. It is a sublime ceremony, an action through which we fully open the storehouse of treasures within. We can thereby tap into the wellspring of life force in the depths of our own beings. We can access the source of inexhaustible wisdom, compassion, and courage.

The universe, in its essence, is Nam-myoho-renge-kyo; our life is an expression of Nam-myoho-renge-kyo; and the Gohonzon is an embodiment of Nam-myoho-renge-kyo. Since all three are Nam-myoho-renge-kyo, they are essentially one and indivisible. Therefore, when we chant Nam-myoho-renge-kyo, our life and the universe are aligned around the Gohonzon—meshing together perfectly like cogs in a machine—and we begin to move in the direction of happiness and fulfillment.

We can be in rhythm with the universe 365 days a year—in spring, summer, autumn, and winter—and manifest the life force, wisdom, and good fortune that enable us to surmount any problem or suffering. When we rev up the powerful engine of life force that is Buddhahood, we can break through any impasse and keep moving forward, boldly steering ourselves in the direction of hope and justice.

Adapted from the dialogue Discussions on Youth, *published in Japanese in March 1999.*

3.2 Chanting Nam-myoho-renge-kyo: A Practice Accessible to All

The vast body of Buddhist teachings sets forth many difficult methods of practice. Nichiren Daishonin, however, insists that all of these diverse Buddhist practices are encompassed in the single practice of chanting Nam-myoho-renge-kyo with faith in the Gohonzon. Here, President Ikeda stresses, based on the Daishonin's writings, that this simple, faith-based practice is the direct path for attaining Buddhahood.

■ Nichiren Daishonin sent many letters to his lay follower Toki Jonin.[21] In one of them, titled "On the Four Stages of Faith and the Five Stages of Practice," he outlines the correct Buddhist practice for people in the Latter Day of the Law, clarifying that such practice lies in "making [the] single word 'faith' the foundation" (see WND-1, 785).

The essence of Nichiren Buddhism is not ritual or formality. It is our heart. It is our faith. The Daishonin further states that the practice of chanting Nam-myoho-renge-kyo with faith in the Gohonzon contains within it all other forms of practice. He explains with the following simple allegory: "The two characters that comprise the name Japan contain within them all the people and animals and wealth in the sixty-six provinces of the country,[22] without a single omission" (WND-1, 788). Similarly, he says, the phrase Nam-myoho-renge-kyo contains within it the entirety of the Lotus Sutra. Therefore, the practice of chanting Nam-myoho-renge-kyo is itself the direct path to attaining Buddhahood. All other practices, especially those entrenched in formality, are secondary practices that, if given primary importance, can become an impediment to faith.

Nichiren further teaches that even though we may not understand the profound meaning of Nam-myoho-renge-kyo, we can still gain the benefit of chanting it. Here, employing another analogy, he states, "When a baby drinks milk, it has no understanding of its taste, and yet its body is naturally nourished" (WND-1, 788).

Though we may not understand Buddhist doctrine, if we simply chant daimoku free of doubt, then, just as a newborn baby gains nourishment from milk, we will naturally be able to imbue our lives with the great power of Nam-myoho-renge-kyo. Nichiren Buddhism is the Buddhism of the people; it exists for and is accessible to all.

In the same writing, Nichiren states: "The five characters of Myoho-renge-kyo[23] do not represent the sutra [Lotus Sutra] text, nor are they its meaning. They are nothing other than the intent of the entire sutra" (WND-1, 788). Nam-myoho-renge-kyo, which we chant, is the heart and essence of the Lotus Sutra. Fundamentally, it is the very spirit of Nichiren Daishonin. Accordingly, though we may not grasp its profound meaning entirely, when we chant with faith in the Gohonzon, we can come into contact with the Daishonin's spirit. We can bring forth within us the life state of the Daishonin that is one with Nam-myoho-renge-kyo. How truly fortunate we are!

From a speech delivered at an SGI-Italy Representatives Conference, Milan, Italy, July 2, 1992.

3.3 Winning in Life With Daimoku

What should our attitude be when chanting Nam-myoho-renge-kyo? In this excerpt from The New Human Revolution, *the novel's protagonist Shin'ichi Yamamoto (whose character represents President Ikeda) is speaking to members in Peru who have just started practicing Nichiren Buddhism. He offers them several pieces of advice, such as: "Firmly resolve to win and chant Nam-myoho-renge-kyo with the power of a lion's roar."*

■ Those who challenge themselves earnestly, aligning their lives with the Mystic Law, kosen-rufu, and the SGI, lay the foundations for eternal happiness and realize ultimate victory in life.

I would like all of you to become such great victors. In that connection, allow me today to talk a little about the key requirements for victory.

The first is chanting Nam-myoho-renge-kyo.

Our health, courage, wisdom, joy, desire to improve, self-discipline, and so on, could all be said to depend on our life force. Chanting Nam-myoho-renge-kyo enables us to bring forth limitless life force. Those who base themselves on chanting Nam-myoho-renge-kyo are therefore never deadlocked.

The important thing is to continue chanting every day, no matter what happens. Nam-myoho-renge-kyo is the fundamental power of the universe. Please chant resounding daimoku morning and evening with the vibrant and energetic rhythm of majestic horses galloping through the heavens.

When we chant before the Gohonzon, we are facing the Buddha, so we should remember to have a respectful attitude. Other than that, though, we should feel free to express what's in our hearts honestly and directly to the Gohonzon.

The Gohonzon is the embodiment of the Buddha endowed with infinite compassion. We should therefore chant about our desires, our problems, and our aspirations, just as they are. When we're suffering, feeling sad, or experiencing hard times, we should take everything to the Gohonzon with an open heart, like a child who throws itself into its mother's arms and clings to her. The Gohonzon will "listen" to everything. Let's chant as if carrying on a conversation, confiding our innermost thoughts. In time, even hellish sufferings will vanish like the morning dew and seem but a dream.

If, for instance, we recognize that we have done something wrong, we should offer sincere prayers of apology and humbly reflect on our behavior. We can resolve never to repeat the same mistake again and set forth anew.

Also, when we encounter a crucial situation, we can firmly resolve to win and chant Nam-myoho-renge-kyo with the power of a lion's roar or the ferocity of an *asura* demon, as if to shake the entire universe.

Furthermore, in the evening, we can joyfully chant to the Gohonzon with profound appreciation for that day.

In *The Record of the Orally Transmitted Teachings*, Nichiren cites the words, "Morning after morning we rise up with the Buddha, evening after evening we lie down with the Buddha"[24] (OTT, 83). This means that those who continue to chant in earnest are always together with the Daishonin, the Buddha of the Latter Day of the Law. This holds true not only for this lifetime, but even beyond death, with the Daishonin and all heavenly deities throughout the universe extending their protection to us. We can therefore feel a deep sense of security from the depths of our being and be free of all fear. We can enjoy and live out our lives with complete confidence.

Chanting transforms suffering into joy and joy into greater joy. That's why it is important for us to single-mindedly chant Nam-myoho-renge-kyo, come what may, whether we are feeling happy or sad, in good times or in bad. This is the direct path to happiness.

Adapted from The New Human Revolution, *volume 11, "Pioneering New Frontiers" chapter, published in Japanese in October 2002.*

3.4 The Significance of the "Expedient Means" and "Life Span" Chapters

Gongyo consists of reciting passages from "Expedient Means" and "Life Span," the second and sixteenth chapters of the Lotus Sutra. Here, President Ikeda discusses the significance of the "Expedient Means" chapter, which teaches that all beings are Buddhas, and the "Life Span" chapter, which describes the philosophy of the eternity of life.

■ I once composed the following poem:

Morning and evening,
joyously attune your lives
to the melody of the universe,
as you recite the "Expedient Means"
and "Life Span" chapters!

What wonderful efforts we are making toward the creation of peace and happiness when we recite these important chapters that comprise the heart of the Lotus Sutra, the highest of all the Buddhist sutras, and vibrantly chant Nam-myoho-renge-kyo, the supreme teaching of Buddhism and ultimate Law of the universe!

The Lotus Sutra was expounded to enable all living beings to attain enlightenment. When read in terms of its implicit meaning—namely, from the doctrinal standpoint of Nichiren Buddhism—the Lotus Sutra takes on profound significance as an "explanation" of the object of devotion (Gohonzon) of Nam-myoho-renge-kyo, the fundamental Law that opens the way for the enlightenment of all living beings throughout the entire world into the eternal future of the Latter Day of the Law.

The essence of this sutra is contained in the "Expedient Means" chapter, which expounds the "true aspect of all phenomena," and in the "Life Span" chapter, which reveals the Buddha's "attainment of Buddhahood in the remote past."

From the standpoint of Nichiren Buddhism, the "Expedient Means" chapter praises the wisdom of Nam-myoho-renge-kyo (the Mystic Law) as infinitely profound and immeasurable, and it elucidates the principle that all living beings are Buddhas. In particular, the section that clarifies the "true aspect of all phenomena" and the "ten factors of life" (the portion that we recite three times during gongyo) indicates that all the ever-changing forms and states of life (all phenomena) are without exception manifestations of Nam-myoho-renge-kyo (the true aspect). The Daishonin writes, "All beings and environments in the Ten Worlds . . . are without exception manifestations of Myoho-renge-kyo" (WND-1, 383). All living beings are inherently entities of the Mystic Law. Therefore, all those who chant Nam-myoho-renge-kyo and work for kosen-rufu are assured of attaining the life state of Buddhahood just as they are.

We don't need to go to some faraway place to attain Buddhahood. We don't need to become someone special. We can commune dynamically with the universe as and where we are and fully reveal the brilliance of our own innate "true aspect"—that is, our true self as an entity of Nam-myoho-renge-kyo. That is the purpose of gongyo and the realm of faith. We can bring forth from within us the wisdom, courage, and compassion of the Mystic Law. We therefore have absolutely nothing to fear.

The term *life span* of "The Life Span of the Thus Come One" chapter contains the meaning of measuring the life span and benefits of the Buddha. Read from the perspective of the meaning implicit in its text, this chapter offers a detailed description of the eternal life span and the benefits of the "Thus Come One Nam-myoho-renge-kyo" (OTT, 123) extending from the infinite past. Here, the eternal nature of life is revealed, along with the fact that this constitutes the true nature of all living beings. Also revealed in this chapter is the mission of the Bodhisattvas of the Earth[25] to spread this great Law and lead all living beings to enlightenment.

The verse section of the "Life Span" chapter, in particular, is a grand paean to the infinitely great, noble, and eternal life force we all possess.

Nichiren notes that when we combine the Chinese character *ji* (self) of the opening line of the verse section—*"ji ga toku burrai"* (Since I attained Buddhahood) —and the final Chinese character *shin* (body) of the closing line—*"soku joju busshin"* (quickly acquire the body of a Buddha), this forms the word *jishin,* meaning "oneself" (see OTT, 140). From beginning to end, the verse section praises the "self" and the "life" of the Buddha, and as such, it is also a paean to the state of eternal and absolute freedom inherent in our lives.

The verse section offers direct answers to the ultimate questions that form the basis of all thought, philosophy, and religion—in other words, the timeless questions of life, such as "What is the meaning of our existence?" "What is the true essence of our being?" "Where have we come from and where are we going?" and "What are life and death?" The verse section comprises a teaching of hope and joy with the power to illuminate all humanity and all life for eternity.

In the verse section, we find the lines: *"Ga shi do annon. Tennin jo juman."* (This, my land, remains safe and tranquil, constantly filled with heavenly and human beings [LSOC, 272]).

There is still immense suffering in the world today—suffering as painful as being "consumed in a great fire" (LSOC, 272). Our noble movement for kosen-rufu, upholding the philosophy of the eternity of life, is firmly committed to creating a world where people live together in happiness and peace—an ideal society that humanity has always longed for. This is the way to secure the right to lead a happy, fulfilled existence for all people in the twenty-first century, an aspiration shared by countless philosophers, religious leaders, and peace scholars.

From a speech delivered at a World Peace Commemorative Gongyo Meeting, Soka Culture Center, Shinanomachi, Tokyo, September 8, 2002.

3.5 Gongyo Purifies Our Lives

In this excerpt, President Ikeda discusses gongyo as the fundamental method for polishing our lives. Through the practice of gongyo, we purify the functions of the six sense organs (eyes, ears, nose, tongue, body, and mind)—our mental and perceptual faculties—and, in so doing, purify our lives.

■ The Mystic Law is the key to polishing our lives. In "On Attaining Buddhahood in This Lifetime," Nichiren Daishonin writes:

> This is similar to a tarnished mirror that will shine like a jewel when polished. A mind now clouded by the illusions of the innate darkness of life is like a tarnished mirror, but when

> polished, it is sure to become like a clear mirror, reflecting the essential nature of phenomena [Dharma nature] and the true aspect of reality. Arouse deep faith, and diligently polish your mirror day and night. How should you polish it? Only by chanting Nam-myoho-renge-kyo. (WND-1, 4)

Our society today is rife with negative influences. People's lives are easily clouded and sullied. That is why we need this fundamental method for polishing and purifying our lives.

A life that has been thoroughly polished [by chanting Nam-myoho-renge-kyo] shines with wisdom, and this wisdom serves as a beacon guiding the way to victory in life. In "The Benefits of the Teacher of the Law," the nineteenth chapter of the Lotus Sutra, the wisdom of those who uphold the Mystic Law is likened to "a pure bright mirror in which forms and shapes are all reflected" (LSOC, 303). Just as a bright, clear mirror reflects every object as it is, a life that has been well polished [by chanting Nam-myoho-renge-kyo] can discern the true reality of all things in the world.

In *The Record of the Orally Transmitted Teachings,* Nichiren comments on this passage:

> The sutra passage is saying that persons whose six sense organs are pure will be like lapis lazuli or like a bright mirror in which one sees the major world system (or the thousand-millionfold world).[26]
>
> Now when Nichiren and his followers chant Nam-myoho-renge-kyo, they see and understand the ten thousand phenomena [i.e., all phenomena],[27] as though these were reflected in a bright mirror. (OTT, 149)

Lapis lazuli is one of the seven kinds of treasures.[28] The purification of the six sense organs[29] is one of the benefits achieved by practitioners of the Mystic Law that is outlined in the "Benefits of the Teacher of the Law" chapter. In other words, through Buddhist practice, we purify and enhance our mental and perceptual faculties as represented by our eyes, ears, nose, tongue, body, and mind—that is, our life in its entirety.

The "bright mirror" of a well-forged and polished life fully reflects the universe, society, and human life. The "bright mirror," fundamentally, is the Gohonzon—in other words, the life of Nichiren Daishonin. In a broader sense, it is the "bright mirror of the single mind [of faith]" (see OTT, 149) of all those who believe in the Gohonzon as disciples of the Daishonin.

This is the profound significance of faith in the Mystic Law. Through strong faith, we can elevate and transform our lives—spiritually and physically—to their purest and strongest possible state. The purification of our lives through faith is the driving force for our victory as human beings. That is why it is vital for us to persevere in faith until the very end of our lives.

From a speech delivered at an Arts Division General Meeting, Soka Culture Center, Shinanomachi, Tokyo, May 10, 1987.

3.6 Change Starts From Prayer

In this excerpt, President Ikeda lectures on Nichiren's writing "On Prayer," in which the Daishonin declares that the prayers of a practitioner of the Lotus Sutra never go unanswered. While explaining that prayer in Nichiren Buddhism is the driving force for carrying out a correct practice, President Ikeda stresses that prayer must also be accompanied by action if we truly seek to transform our lives.

■ Nichiren Daishonin writes:

> The prayers offered by a practitioner of the Lotus Sutra will be answered just as an echo answers a sound, as a shadow follows a form, as the reflection of the moon appears in clear water, as a mirror collects dewdrops,[30] as a magnet attracts iron, as amber attracts particles of dust, or as a clear mirror reflects the color of an object. (WND-1, 340)

In this passage, he states that the prayers of the votary of the Lotus Sutra are always answered. His use of natural principles and phenomena as analogies demonstrates his strong confidence in what he is saying.

Wherever practitioners of the Lotus Sutra chant Nam-myoho-renge-kyo, just as an echo answers a sound and a shadow follows a form, their prayers will unfailingly produce positive results there. The Daishonin teaches that our lives are transformed—both spiritually and physically—by prayer, which in turn exerts a positive influence on our environment.

Prayer is not something abstract. Many today may regard the intangible, unseen realm of life as nothing more than a product of the imagination. But if we were to view things only from a material perspective, then our relationships with people and things would largely appear to arise solely from the chaos of randomness. The penetrating insight of Buddhism, however, discerns the Law of life in the depths of chaos and apprehends it as the force that supports and activates all phenomena from within.

Nichiren writes: "As life does not go beyond the moment, the Buddha expounded the blessings that come from a single moment of rejoicing [on hearing the Lotus Sutra]"[31] (WND-1, 62). Because "life does not go beyond the moment," as he says, our focus should be on the power that emerges from within us at each moment to support us and give fundamental direction to our lives. Prayer—namely chanting Nam-myoho-renge-kyo—is the only way for us to confront on this fundamental level the delusions inherent in life.

It thus follows that prayer is the driving force for maintaining a correct practice and tenacious action. Nothing is as insubstantial as action without prayer. For those who neglect prayer, things may appear to go quite smoothly for a while. They may even seem very upbeat. But once faced with adversity, they tend to fall into despair, their lives as fragile as a withered tree. Lacking self-mastery, they are tossed about like leaves on the turbulent waters of society.

The path up the hill of life doesn't follow a straight line. There are successes and mistakes. Sometimes we win and sometimes we lose. With each step on our way, with every curve and corner we navigate, we grow a little bit more. In this process, prayer functions as a powerful force preventing us from becoming arrogant in victory or devastated by defeat.

That's why none are stronger than those who base themselves on prayer. Our strong, focused prayer manifests as the power of faith and practice, which in turn activates the power of the Buddha and the Law. The main player in this drama is always the human being—it is we ourselves.

Prayer produces a change within our hearts, within the depths of our lives. This profound, intangible inner change does not end with us alone [but inspires a similar change in others]. Likewise, when one community changes, it will not be limited to that community alone. Just as a single wave gives rise to countless others, change in one community will create a ripple effect of change in other communities as well.

I wish to assert that the first step toward such social change is a change in the heart of a single individual.

This is also, I believe, where the deep significance of the Daishonin's statement that "Buddhism is reason" (WND-1, 839) lies.

To return to the passage from "On Prayer" that we are studying, "sound," "form," and "clear water" correspond to our attitude in prayer, while "echo," "shadow," and "reflection of the moon" correspond to the natural way in which prayers are answered. Just as these three analogies refer to phenomena that arise in accord with natural principles, the prayers of a practitioner of the Lotus Sutra will also be definitely answered in accord with the inexorable Law of life and in accord with reason.

Prayer in Nichiren Buddhism is free of all arrogance and conceit. The very act of sitting before the Gohonzon and chanting Nam-myoho-renge-kyo pulses with the humble spirit to transcend attachment to one's own shallow wisdom and limited experience to become one with the Law of life and the fundamental rhythm of nature and the universe, which were revealed through the Buddha's enlightened wisdom. Without being self-abasing, we concentrate all our actions into a single life moment—into our determined prayer—while recharging our lives to prepare for boundless, vibrant growth. That is the healthiest and most fulfilling state of life.

Let us chant to the Gohonzon about all our problems in life and challenge them.

Prayer is essential. Let's never forget that everything starts from prayer. If we lose sight of prayer and fail to transform our lives in actuality, then even the most eloquent speeches and high-minded arguments will all be just empty theory, pipe dreams, and illusions. Faith and the Soka Gakkai spirit, too, arise from praying strongly and deeply about our actual situations and realities.

In Nichiren Buddhism, prayer by itself isn't enough. Just as an arrow flying toward its target contains the full power and strength of the archer who shot it, our prayer contains all our efforts and actions. Prayer without action is just wishful thinking, and action without prayer will be unproductive.

I therefore would like to point out that lofty prayer arises from a lofty sense of responsibility. Serious prayer will not arise from an irresponsible or careless attitude toward work, daily living, and life itself. Those who take responsibility for every part of their lives and give their all in every endeavor will make a habit of prayer.

Living in society can be difficult, so I hope you will deal with every aspect of your lives based on strong prayer.

Adapted from a lecture on Nichiren Daishonin's writing "On Prayer," published in the October 22, 1977, Seikyo Shimbun.

3.7 Daimoku: Quality or Quantity?

Here, President Ikeda responds to a question from an Italian member about whether quantity or quality is more important in chanting Nam-myoho-renge-kyo. Pointing out that Buddhist practice is not about rules and formality, President Ikeda says that we should chant and act in a way that creates value and gives us a sense of satisfaction and fulfillment.

■ A 100,000-lira note is worth more than a 10,000-lira note. It goes without saying that it is preferable to have the note with the greater value. In the case of chanting Nam-myoho-renge-kyo, the important thing is to chant earnestly and with strong conviction. Of course, it would be even better to have lots of 100,000-lira notes! The bottom line is that both quality and quantity matter in chanting.

The principle of "responsive communion" is very important in Nichiren Buddhism. To use an analogy, when talking on the phone, if the connection is good, we'll be heard even if we speak softly, but if it's bad, then sometimes the other person won't be able to hear us even if we shout. For our prayers to be effective, we need to express them honestly and directly to the Gohonzon.

The Daishonin states, "What is called faith is nothing unusual" (WND-1, 1036). In other words, we can just be ourselves. He continues:

> Faith means putting one's trust in the Lotus Sutra, Shakyamuni, Many Treasures, the Buddhas and bodhisattvas of the ten directions, and the heavenly gods and benevolent deities, and chanting Nam-myoho-renge-kyo as a woman cherishes her husband, as a man lays down his life for his wife, as parents refuse to abandon their children, or as a child refuses to leave its mother. (WND-1, 1036)

We should be honest and unpretentious when we chant to the Gohonzon. If we are suffering or feeling sad, then we should take that suffering to the Gohonzon without hiding it, expressing in our prayers what is in our hearts.

It is the Daishonin's wish that we all become happy. By coming in contact with and connecting with the life of the Daishonin [by chanting to the Gohonzon], therefore, we are certain to attain happiness. It is inconceivable that the Daishonin would fail to protect those who are striving as his emissaries to realize kosen-rufu.

Essentially, we practice Nichiren Buddhism for our own happiness and well-being. In chanting, too, the main thing is that we ourselves feel happy and satisfied. It's not a matter of formality; there are no rules specifying how long we have to chant and so on. While it is often helpful to set ourselves a target for the amount we want to chant, when we're too tired or sleepy, or we find ourselves dozing off in front of the Gohonzon and just chanting out of force of habit, then it is far more valuable to get some rest and chant properly another time, when we're refreshed in body and mind.

The most important thing is that we are filled with a satisfying sense of revitalization after chanting. When we continue chanting in this way each day, we will naturally come to experience a life in which all our desires are fulfilled.

From remarks at a question-and-answer session during the North Italy Representative Leaders Meeting commemorating July 3, Mentor-Disciple Day, Milan Community Center, Milan, Italy, July 3, 1992.

3.8 Chanting Nam-myoho-renge-kyo Enables Us to Lead the Most Meaningful Lives

In this excerpt, President Ikeda responds to the question of a member who asked: "When we were chanting together with you earlier, the desire and courage to realize my dreams came welling forth from my life. How can I chant with this kind of feeling and live with courage all the time?" President Ikeda also emphasizes that as long as we persevere in faith, we will be able to lead the most meaningful lives.

■ Even one daimoku can pervade the entire universe. Truly heartfelt and determined prayer, therefore, has the power to move everything.

To illustrate, the words "I love you" can have a completely different impact depending on whether they are said from the heart or merely as an empty gesture.

Chanting with the deep conviction that one's life is the entity of the Mystic Law, or with the resolve to dedicate one's life to spreading the Mystic Law as an emissary of the Buddha, cannot fail to resonate with the Gohonzon or reach the universe. A person who chants in this way will definitely attain a state of complete freedom.

Of course, no one becomes an expert in anything right away. It is by overcoming obstacles again and again, and continuing to press forward, that we gain a degree of expertise or mastery in a given field.

The same holds true for faith. There may be times when we give in to self-defeat and our determination wanes, or when things don't go as we'd hoped and we begin to feel anxious or fearful. But the important thing is to continue chanting, no matter what. Whether our prayers are answered right away or not, we must keep chanting Nam-myoho-renge-kyo, without harboring any doubts. Those who maintain such faith will eventually attain the supreme path and highest pinnacle of value and savor the conviction that everything unfolded in the very best and most meaningful way. They will build immensely fulfilling lives and come to regard everything as a source of joy and a part of their mission. Such are the workings of the Mystic Law and the power of faith.

Why is the Gohonzon important? Because, through having faith in it, we can bring forth the Gohonzon, or the state of Buddhahood, that is inherent in our own lives. The Daishonin states that the Gohonzon is found only in the faith of each one of us (see WND-1, 832).

We ourselves and all human beings are worthy of respect because every single individual is an entity of the Mystic Law. The Gohonzon is important above all because it enables us to manifest the Mystic Law that exists within us.

From remarks at a question-and-answer session during the North Italy Representative Leaders Meeting commemorating July 3, Mentor-Disciple Day, Milan Community Center, Milan, Italy, July 3, 1992.

3.9 Develop a Strong Inner Core

Here, President Ikeda responds to the concern of a future division member who was failing to make any headway in solving a difficult problem even after having decided to challenge it by earnestly doing gongyo every day. He explains that in Nichiren Buddhism, no prayer goes unanswered, but that the benefits we accrue from faith in the Gohonzon are sometimes conspicuous and sometimes inconspicuous. So even if we do not see concrete results immediately from our practice, it's important that we continue to persevere in chanting and making efforts. If we do so, he says, we can move in the direction that is the very best for us.

■ In Nichiren Buddhism, it is said that no prayer goes unanswered. But this is very different from having every wish instantly gratified as if by magic. If you chant to win the lottery tomorrow, or score 100 percent on a test tomorrow without having studied, the odds are small that it will happen. Nonetheless, viewed from a deeper, longer-term perspective, all your prayers serve to propel you in the direction of happiness.

Sometimes our immediate prayers are realized, and sometimes they aren't. When we look back later, however, we can say with absolute conviction that everything turned out for the best.

Buddhism accords with reason. Our faith is manifested in our daily lives, in our actual circumstances. Our prayers cannot be answered if we fail to make efforts to realize them.

Furthermore, it takes a great deal of time and effort to overcome sufferings of a karmic nature, whose roots lie deep in causes we made in the past. There is a big difference, for example, in the time it takes for a scratch to heal and that required to recover from a serious internal disease. Some illnesses can be treated with medication, while others require surgery. The same applies to changing our karma through faith and practice.

In addition, each person's level of faith and individual karma differ. By chanting Nam-myoho-renge-kyo, however, we can bring forth a powerful sense of hope and move our lives in a positive, beneficial direction without fail.

It's unrealistic to think we can achieve anything of substance overnight. If we were to have every prayer answered instantly, it would lead to our ruin. We'd grow lazy and complacent.

You may have a passing interest in painting, for example. But if you think you can simply dash off some paintings, suddenly hold an exhibition, and have your work snapped up by art collectors, you are hardly being realistic.

Suppose you spend all your money playing rather than working and are now destitute. Do you think someone giving you a large sum of money would contribute to your happiness in the long term?

It would be like making superficial repairs to a crumbling building without addressing the root problem. To create something fine and solid, it would be better to build anew from the foundation up. The purpose of our Buddhist practice is to transform our lives on a fundamental level, not superficially. It enables us to develop a strong inner core and solidly accumulate indestructible good fortune.

There are two kinds of benefit that derive from faith in the Gohonzon: conspicuous and inconspicuous. Conspicuous benefit is the obvious, visible benefit of being protected or being quickly able to surmount a problem when it arises—be it an illness or a conflict in personal relationships.

Inconspicuous benefit, on the other hand, is less tangible. It is good fortune accumulated slowly but steadily, like the growth of a tree or the rising of the tide, which results in the forging of a rich and expansive state of life. We might not discern any change from day to day, but as the years pass, it will be clear that we've become happy, that we've grown as individuals. This is inconspicuous benefit.

When you chant Nam-myoho-renge-kyo, you will definitely gain the best result, regardless of whether that benefit is conspicuous or inconspicuous.

No matter what happens, the important thing is to continue chanting. If you do so, you'll become happy without fail. Even if things don't work out the way you hoped or imagined, when you look back later, you'll understand on a much more profound level that it was the best possible result. This is tremendous inconspicuous benefit.

Conspicuous benefit, for instance, might allow you to eat your fill today but leave you worrying about your next meal. As an example of inconspicuous benefit, on the other hand, you may have only a meager meal today but you are moving steadily toward a life in which you will never have to worry about having enough to eat. The latter is a far more attractive prospect, I think, and is the essence of practicing Nichiren Buddhism.

Adapted from the dialogue Discussion on Youth, *published in Japanese in March 1999.*

3.10 Gongyo and Daimoku: Our Daily "Spiritual Workout"

In this excerpt, President Ikeda responds to the concern of future division members who feel guilty when they don't do gongyo.

Explaining that the purpose of Buddhism is to free us, not to constrain us, he says that the spirit to keep challenging oneself, even if only a little, is truly admirable.

■ As long as we have faith in the Gohonzon, we are not going to suffer punishment or negative consequences from missing gongyo, so please put your mind at ease. Nichiren says that chanting Nam-myoho-renge-kyo even once is a source of limitless benefit. So imagine the immense benefit you will accumulate when you continue earnestly to recite the sutra and chant Nam-myoho-renge-kyo morning and evening. It is something we do for our own sake; it is a right, not an obligation.

The Gohonzon will never demand that you chant to it. Having appreciation for being able to chant to the Gohonzon is the heart of faith. The more you exert yourselves in faith—reciting the sutra and chanting Nam-myoho-renge-kyo—the more you stand to gain.

Also, Nichiren writes nothing about the specific amount we should chant. It is entirely up to each individual's awareness. Faith is a lifelong pursuit, so there's no need to be unnecessarily nervous or anxious about how much you chant.

You don't have to put unnecessary pressure on yourselves. Buddhism exists to free people, not to restrain them. Chanting every day, even a little bit, is important. For instance, the food you eat each day turns into energy that fuels your bodies. Your studies, too, become a valuable asset when you make steady efforts on a daily basis.

Our lives are created from what we do and how we live every day. For that reason, we should strive to live each day so as to continually improve ourselves. The driving force for this is our morning and evening gongyo.

Exerting ourselves in the practice of gongyo each day amounts to what we might call a "spiritual workout." It purifies our lives, gets our "motors" running, and sets us on the right track. It gets our bodies and minds moving and sets a good rhythm for the day.

It is important to have the spirit to sit down in front of the Gohonzon. The spirit to keep challenging yourself to pray before the Gohonzon every day, to chant, even if only a little, is truly admirable.

Adapted from the dialogue Discussions on Youth, *published in Japanese in March 1999.*

3.11 Our Prayer Reaches the Buddhas and Bodhisattvas of the Ten Directions

Here, President Ikeda responds to a question from a member about the effectiveness of reciting passages from the Lotus Sutra and chanting in a language one doesn't understand. He stresses that whether we understand the words or not, they are the language of the realm of Buddhas and bodhisattvas. They are understood by the Gohonzon and communicated to all the Buddhas and bodhisattvas of the universe, and enable us to attain great happiness, fulfillment, and joy.

■ I would like to address the question of whether there is any value in reciting sutra passages and chanting Nam-myoho-renge-kyo without understanding their meaning.

Of course, it is better if you understand their meaning. That will strengthen your faith in the Mystic Law. But if you understand and yet fail to practice, it won't get you anywhere. Moreover, you cannot understand all of the profound significance of the Law through reason alone.

Birds and dogs, for example, have their own language, their own speech. People do not understand it, but other birds and dogs do. There are many comparable examples among humans as well—codes, abbreviations, or foreign languages that are comprehended by experts or native speakers but unintelligible to others. Married couples also sometimes have their own language that only they understand!

In the same way, the language of the sutra and daimoku reaches the Gohonzon and the realms of the Buddhas and bodhisattvas of the ten directions and three existences. We might call it the language of the Buddhas and bodhisattvas. That is why our voices reciting the sutra and chanting Nam-myoho-renge-kyo to the Gohonzon reach all Buddhas, bodhisattvas, and heavenly deities, whether we understand what we are saying or not. They hear it and say in response, "Excellent, excellent!" rejoicing and praising us. The entire universe envelops us in the light of happiness.

Nichiren teaches that through reciting the sutra and chanting Nam-myoho-renge-kyo, we can reach an elevated state of life in which, while engaged in our daily activities, we freely traverse the cosmos. In "Reply to Sairen-bo," the Daishonin writes: "Those who are our disciples and lay supporters can view Eagle Peak in India and day and night will go to and from the Land of Eternally Tranquil Light that has existed for all time. What a truly inexpressible joy it is!" (WND-1, 313).

When we chant to the Gohonzon, the door to our inner microcosm instantly opens to the macrocosm of the entire universe, and we savor a serene and boundless happiness, as if gazing out over the entire cosmos. We feel a deep fulfillment and joy along with a feeling of supreme confidence and self-mastery, as if we hold everything in the palm of our hands. The microcosm enfolded by the macrocosm reaches out to enfold the macrocosm in its own embrace.

The Daishonin writes in "Letter to Niike", "When nurtured by the chanting of Nam-myoho-renge-kyo . . . , [we] are free to soar into the sky of the true aspect of all phenomena" (WND-1, 1030).

In "On Offerings for Deceased Ancestors," he also says: "Though he himself is like the wisteria vine, because he clings to the pine that is the Lotus Sutra, he is able to ascend the mountain of perfect enlightenment. Because he has the wings of the single vehicle [Mystic Law] to rely upon, he can soar into the sky of Tranquil Light [Buddhahood]" (WND-1, 821).

Just as we might climb the highest mountain peak to gaze down on the bright, clear scene of the world below, we can climb the mountain of perfect enlightenment, or supreme wisdom, the Daishonin says. We can attain a state of eternal bliss, experiencing moment after moment the infinite expanse and depth of life, as if soaring through the universe and savoring the sight of myriad beautiful stars, blazing comets, and glittering galaxies.

From a speech delivered at an SGI-USA Youth Training Session, Malibu Training Center, California, February 20, 1990.

CHAPTER 4

Transforming Suffering Into Joy

Introduction to the Chapter:

Faith is another name for infinite hope.

No life is without problems and suffering. The question is how do we deal with the seemingly unending trials and tribulations that assail us? Do we avert our gaze and run away from them? Do we just accept them with a fatalistic sense of resignation? Or do we hold on to hope and face them head-on, rising to the challenges they present? The key to leading a happy life depends on which of these attitudes we adopt.

In his writings, Nichiren Daishonin uses Buddhist concepts and principles to teach us that rather than trying to escape troubles, we should courageously confront them, seeing them as opportunities to develop the lofty life state of Buddhahood.

For example, the principle that "earthly desires lead to enlightenment" tells us that instead of eliminating earthly desires, the deluded impulses that cause us suffering, we can use them to bring forth enlightenment. The principle of "changing poison into medicine" teaches that we can transform suffering (poison) into the supreme happiness of the life state of Buddhahood (medicine). The principle of "lessening karmic retribution" teaches, based on the Buddhist perspective of the eternity of life, that we can lessen any negative consequences we might stand to incur as a result of negative actions committed in past existences, underscoring the importance of changing our karma in this lifetime.

In this chapter, based on such principles, President Ikeda stresses that the greater the suffering and hardship we encounter, the greater the joy and happiness we can transform them into through our strong practice of Nichiren Buddhism.

4.1 We Are the Protagonists of Our Own Triumphant Dramas

How can we overcome our problems and lead victorious lives? In this excerpt, President Ikeda discusses an active life philosophy grounded in the Buddhist principle of "three thousand realms in a single moment of life," which ultimately means that each of us writes the script and plays the leading role in the triumphant drama of our own life.

■ We are each the scriptwriter of our own triumphant drama. We are also its protagonist. Shakespeare writes: "All the world's a stage/ And all the men and women merely players."[32]

Buddhism teaches us that we each write and perform the script of our own life. No one else writes that script for us. We write it, and we are the star who performs it. This extremely active life philosophy is inherent in the teachings of "three thousand realms in a single moment of life."

We are each the author and main character of our own story.

For it to be a wonderful production, it's essential that we become so familiar with the scenario that we can picture it vividly. We may need to rehearse it mentally. Sometimes it helps to write down our goals (for example, to pass an examination or to improve at work), and read them over and over again until they are deeply impressed in our minds.

There once was a young boy who had an accident that left one of his legs shorter than the other. His parents, however, never told him that anything was too hard or impossible for him to do. They treated him like any other child and encouraged him to play sports. They taught him that he could do whatever he believed he could, and that if he was unable to do something, it was because he had decided he couldn't before even trying. Their conviction wasn't based on mere idealism or optimism. It was a belief in the latent potential of the human being.

The boy later became a star football player at school, and after graduation he succeeded in society as well. His life perfectly illustrates the following assertion, made by the Russian writer Maksim Gorky in one of his novels: "Talent is nothing but faith in yourself, in your own powers."[33]

Sir Walter Scott, the great Scottish author, wrote, "To the timid and hesitating everything is impossible, because it seems so."[34]

Thinking "It's impossible" or "It can't be done" has the effect of actually making anything and everything impossible. Similarly, if parents constantly tell their children they are hopeless or inept, the children will come to believe it and may wind up fulfilling that expectation.

Nichiren Daishonin cites a passage from the Flower Garland Sutra:

> The mind is like a skilled painter, who creates various forms made up of the five components.[35] Thus of all the phenomena throughout the entire world, there is not a single one

> that is not created by the mind. . . . Outside of this mind there is no other phenomenon that exists. (WND-2, 844)

When we read the Daishonin's letters, we find that he constantly cites sutras and Buddhist scriptures to offer examples and documentary proof relevant to the situations or questions of the recipients, seeking to change their hearts, strengthen their determination, and give them conviction and self-confidence. His words always radiate hope and encouragement, like the sun. This is because he fully understood that when a person's heart changes, everything changes.

Many people ascribe others' success to favorable circumstances. They are likely to think, "If only I had such good luck" or "If only I didn't have this problem to deal with." But that ultimately is just complaining. There is no one who doesn't have problems.

A businessman once said to a friend: "You're always complaining about having so many problems. I know a place where there are at least ten thousand people, and not one of them has even a single problem or worry. Would you like me to take you there?"

His friend said, "Yes, please do!"

And guess where the businessman took him? To a cemetery. He was teaching his friend that as long as we are alive, we will have to deal with problems and sufferings. Challenging ourselves to find ways to overcome these problems gives richness and meaning to our lives.

Buddhism teaches that earthly desires lead to enlightenment. This means the greater our worries and sufferings, the greater the happiness we can transform them into through the power of chanting Nam-myoho-renge-kyo.

In Shakyamuni's day, there was a woman who had lost her beloved child to illness. Half insane with grief, she wandered the town clutching her dead child to her bosom and begged all those she encountered, "Please give me medicine for my child."

Feeling pity for her, someone took her to see Shakyamuni. When he heard her story, he said: "Do not fret. I will give you good medicine. Go into the town and bring me back some mustard seeds. But they must be mustard seeds from a family where no one has lost a loved one."

In her quest, the woman walked all over the town, going from door to door. But there was not one family that had not lost a loved one. Finally, it dawned on her: All human beings die. She was not alone in her suffering. To gain insight into the eternity of life, she became a follower of Shakyamuni, and she later came to be respected as a sage.[36]

By employing the expedient means of sending her out in search of mustard seeds, Shakyamuni freed and restored peace to the heart of this woman who had been wrapped up in her own grief. He helped her awaken to a deeper wisdom based on the eternity of life.

The most important thing is to expand our state of life. When we think only of ourselves, we become increasingly caught up in our small egos, or lesser selves. In contrast, when we work toward a great and all-encompassing objective—for the sake of the Law, the happiness of others, and the welfare of society—we can develop big hearts and bring forth our greater selves through the "wonderful workings of one mind" (OTT, 30). With big hearts, we can savor truly immense happiness. Sufferings that may have once been a heavy burden in a lesser state of life will appear minor, and we can calmly rise above them. I hope all of you will lead lives in which you can demonstrate such brilliant, positive proof of the "wonderful workings of one mind."

From a speech delivered at the SGI-USA Representatives Conference in Miami, Florida, March 9, 1993.

4.2 "Earthly Desires Lead to Enlightenment"

Many think that happiness is the absence of problems and suffering. Nichiren Daishonin discusses the Buddhist principle that "earthly desires lead to enlightenment," saying: "[When Nichiren and his followers recite Nam-myoho-renge-kyo], they are burning the firewood of earthly desires, summoning up the wisdom fire of bodhi or enlightenment" (OTT, 11). Based on this principle, President Ikeda tells us that when we chant Nam-myoho-renge-kyo with strong faith in the Mystic Law, we can transform any kind of problem or suffering into fuel for our happiness.

■ Buddhism teaches the principle that "earthly desires lead to enlightenment." To explain this very simply, "earthly desires" refers to suffering and to the desires and cravings that cause suffering, while "enlightenment" refers to happiness and an enlightened state of life.

Normally, one would assume that earthly desires and enlightenment are separate and independent conditions—especially since suffering would seem to be the exact opposite of happiness. But this is not the case in Nichiren Buddhism, which teaches that only by burning the "firewood" of problems and suffering can we obtain the "flames" of happiness. In other words, by using suffering as fuel, we gain the "light" and "energy" for happiness. And it is by chanting Nam-myoho-renge-kyo that we "burn the firewood of earthly desires."

When we chant Nam-myoho-renge-kyo, our problems and sufferings all turn into energy for our happiness, into fuel that enables us to keep moving forward in our lives.

The wonderful thing about faith in Nichiren Buddhism is that it enables those who suffer the most to attain the greatest happiness and those who experience the most daunting problems to lead the most wonderful, meaningful lives.

Problems come in all shapes and sizes. You may be dealing with some personal problem, you may be wondering how to help your parents live long and fulfilling lives, or you may be worried about friends who are sick or depressed and wish for their recovery. On a different level, you may be deeply concerned about the issue of world peace or the direction of the world in the twenty-first century. These are very noble concerns.

Through chanting Nam-myoho-renge-kyo, you can turn all these worries and concerns into fuel to propel yourselves forward—you can transform them into life force, into greater depth of character, and into good fortune. I therefore hope you will challenge all kinds of problems, chant abundantly about them, and develop yourselves along the way.

Faith means setting goals and striving to achieve each one. If we view each goal or challenge as a mountain, faith is a process whereby we grow with every mountain climbed.

Adapted from the dialogue Discussions on Youth, *published in Japanese in March 1999.*

4.3 "Changing Poison Into Medicine"

Buddhism teaches the principle of "changing poison into medicine." In this excerpt, President Ikeda shows how, through practicing Nichiren Buddhism, we can change the "poison" of problems and suffering into "medicine" and adorn our lives with ultimate victory.

■ Life inevitably involves victory and defeat. There may be times of sorrow and suffering. But Buddhism teaches that "earthly desires lead to enlightenment" and "the sufferings of life and death lead to nirvana." The greater our problems and suffering, the greater the joy and happiness we can transform them into through our Buddhist practice.

We practice this Buddhism for our own sake. The purpose of our faith and practice is to live true to ourselves. It is to increase our good fortune and open the way to happiness. Since this is the case, if we are easily swayed by trifling matters, upbeat one minute and down the next, we cannot say that we are truly practicing Nichiren Buddhism.

In the realm of the Mystic Law, no matter what happens, we can, in time, positively transform all poison into medicine.

In fact, there is really no clear-cut dividing line between poison and medicine. The same substance can act as either a poison or a medicine, depending on the dosage and the life force of the individual who takes it. Some have even described medicine as "poison that saves lives."

Similarly, there is no clear difference between what will function as poison or medicine when it comes to victory and defeat in life. For instance, if we triumph in the end, everything we experienced can be seen as medicine. On the other hand, if our lives end in defeat, then everything—even that which seemed to function as medicine along the way—becomes poison.

What do we mean by triumphing in the end? It means being victorious in faith. For this is our true victory as a human being—one that leads to our victory throughout the three existences of past, present, and future.

From a speech delivered at a chapter leaders meeting, Tokyo, July 27, 1989.

4.4 Creating the Future With the Buddhism of True Cause

Buddhism teaches the causality of life, explaining that our past actions are causes that manifest themselves as positive or negative effects in the present. But overemphasizing this view can lead to focusing too much on the past and developing a passive or fatalistic attitude toward life. In this section, President Ikeda clarifies that Nichiren Buddhism teaches the great principle of true cause, which allows us to always move forward into the future from the present moment on, unconstrained by the past.

■ It often seems that people begin to seriously consider the nature of cause and effect or what it means to lead a happy life only when they experience acute suffering themselves. When all is going smoothly, they tend not to give much thought to the truly important things in life. In that sense, difficulties play a crucial role in helping us lead deeper and more meaningful lives. In fact, that's how we should look at them.

No life is utterly without problems or difficulties. All too often, seemingly happy life circumstances can become a cause of suffering and unhappiness. This is something we come to recognize more and more as we mature in years and experience.

A married couple's happiness, for instance, may be shattered when their child is born with a serious illness. All sorts of unanticipated events can assail us—a sudden economic downturn, a fire or accident, family discord, divorce, difficult personal relationships. They can even sometimes lead to lifelong suffering. It is truly the case that we never know what tomorrow brings. None can declare with certainty that they will never encounter misfortune.

Even those who enjoy security and tranquillity can come to feel that their lives have no meaning as they age. There are still others who always seem to be busily engaged in purposeful endeavors but are in reality simply trying to escape loneliness and emptiness by doing so, unwilling to reflect on themselves or their lives.

Behind a smile might lie sadness. After pleasure might come emptiness. Problems and suffering are inescapable realities of life. And yet, we must go on living. How, then, should we live? How can we change suffering into true joy? The Buddhism of Nichiren Daishonin has the answer to these important and fundamental questions.

Nichiren Buddhism is the Buddhism of true cause.[37] It is a great, revolutionary teaching. It reveals that Nam-myoho-renge-kyo is the fundamental cause for attaining enlightenment and that, by simply embracing the Gohonzon, we can acquire in this lifetime all the practices and virtues of the Buddha.[38]

The Daishonin's teaching focuses on the present and the future. Its essence is for us to always keep advancing while looking toward and brightly illuminating the future.

Practicing this Buddhism doesn't mean that problems and suffering disappear. The reality of life is that, within any of the Ten Worlds, the other nine are always present—hence, the nine worlds characterized by delusion and suffering also exist within the world of Buddhahood. Likewise, the world of Buddhahood can express itself only within the reality of the other nine worlds.

The important thing is to remain undaunted when difficulties arise, to firmly believe that they are expressions of the Buddha's compassion and forge ahead with even stronger faith.

Some may weakly succumb to doubt and question why they still have problems even though they are practicing Nichiren Buddhism. But such a weak way of thinking will—in accord with the principle of three thousand realms in a single moment of life—come to permeate every aspect of their lives and create a state of even greater suffering. This is the opposite of having strong faith.

As ordinary people, we may not be able to fathom why a particular event happens at a particular time, but over the long term we will come to understand its meaning. We will also be able to positively transform the situation, changing poison into medicine. I can say this with complete confidence based on my personal experience of more than four decades of Buddhist practice. We may not understand the significance of a certain event until five or ten years later, or it may even take a lifetime. But from the perspective of the eternity of life spanning the three existences, everything has meaning as an expression of the Buddha wisdom.

From a speech delivered at a Nationwide Youth Division Leaders Meeting, Tokyo, April 29, 1988.

4.5 Living With Joy Throughout All

The ability to transform everything in life into a source of joy is the mark of an expert in the art of living. Here, President Ikeda explains that there is no better way to live than to face every challenge and obstacle with a positive, joyful spirit.

■ Leo Tolstoy exclaimed: "Rejoice! Rejoice! The business of life, its purpose, is joy. Rejoice at the sky, the sun, the stars, the grass, the trees, animals, people."[39]

"Rejoice!"—that was one of the ultimate conclusions the great Russian writer and thinker reached in life.

Living with joy throughout all is the hallmark of a lofty state of being, of strength and happiness. In contrast, a life that greets everything with criticism and complaint is miserable, no matter how fine it might look from the outside.

In 1901, Tolstoy was excommunicated by the Russian Orthodox Church. He was seventy-two at the time, already advanced in years. The Church thought that taking this punitive measure would humiliate Tolstoy, who was widely admired around the world. But he was unruffled by the tactics of the Church authorities. He observed their actions with serene dignity.

"Rejoice, rejoice!" His conviction remained unshaken. In fact, he burned with a passionate fighting spirit.

Tolstoy's life was not untroubled. He struggled with his writing, with unhappiness in his family life, and with illness. But his spirit was to always and everywhere seek out and create joy.

This is also the Buddhist way of life. I hope you will all lead lives of pursuing and creating joy.

Nichiren Daishonin declared: "Nam-myoho-renge-kyo is the greatest of all joys" (OTT, 212). A life dedicated to kosen-rufu is a life of supreme joy. He also wrote:

> I feel immeasurable delight even though I am now an exile. (WND-1, 386)

* * * *

> The more the government authorities rage against me, the greater is my joy. (WND-1, 243)

* * * *

> The greater the hardships befalling [the votary of the Lotus Sutra], the greater the delight he feels, because of his strong faith. (WND-1, 33)

And at the time of the Tatsunokuchi Persecution, the Daishonin said to his loyal disciple Shijo Kingo, who accompanied him, "What greater joy could there be?" (WND-1, 767). "You should smile!" he was telling him.

When hardships occur, he taught, "The wise will rejoice while the foolish will retreat" (WND-1, 637).

The more challenges we face, the more joyfully we should move forward and the more determinedly we should tackle them—this is the essence of Nichiren Buddhism and the most valuable way to lead our lives.

A joyless life is miserable. Those who are put off by everything, who are always negative, wear pained expressions, and do nothing but criticize and complain are not living as the Daishonin teaches in his writings.

Those who can find joy in everything, who can transform everything into joy, are genuine experts in the art of living.

In "Letter from Sado" Nichiren writes, "Worthies and sages are tested by abuse" (WND-1, 303). Truly great individuals are distinguished by their ability to endure criticism and abuse and calmly lead joyful lives.

Finding joy in everything—when you brim with joy, you will lift the spirits of those around you, bring smiles to people's faces, and create value.

It is vital above all that leaders constantly think about how they can enable everyone to advance with joy.

From a speech delivered at a Divisional Representatives Meeting, Tokyo, June 28, 1993.

4.6 Both Suffering and Joy Are a Part of Life

In life, there are times of smooth sailing and rough sailing. Citing encouragement that Nichiren Daishonin offered his disciple Shijo Kingo in a time of adversity, President Ikeda explains the importance of establishing an elevated state of life that enables us to calmly surmount all obstacles, without being swayed by immediate events and circumstances.

■ I would like to share a passage that I'm sure all of you are very familiar with. It is from a letter of encouragement that Nichiren Daishonin sent to Shijo Kingo, who found himself in difficult circumstances. Kingo had incurred his lord's disfavor by trying to convert him to Nichiren's teaching, an act that also invited hostility from his fellow samurai retainers. Nichiren writes to him:

> Suffer what there is to suffer, enjoy what there is to enjoy. Regard both suffering and joy as facts of life, and continue chanting Nam-myoho-renge-kyo, no matter what happens. How could this be anything other than [experiencing] the boundless joy of the Law? Strengthen your power of faith more than ever. (WND-1, 681)

Right now, your life may be filled with suffering. But just as pleasure never lasts forever, neither does suffering. In life, there is both suffering and joy. Sometimes we win, and other times we lose. Both suffering and joy are a part of life; this is life's reality. That is why, whether experiencing suffering or joy, we should keep chanting

Nam-myoho-renge-kyo, just as we are, says the Daishonin. If we do that, we will attain a state of supreme happiness through the wisdom and power of the Mystic Law. We can lead a life in which nothing will defeat us.

Nichiren uses the phrase "experiencing the boundless joy of the Law." "Experiencing" here means that we obtain and savor this joy ourselves. It comes down to us, not others. This joy is not bestowed on us by someone else or something outside ourselves. Creating our own happiness and experiencing that happiness for ourselves; developing the inner strength and capacity to serenely enjoy life, regardless of its ups and downs—this is the meaning of "experiencing the boundless joy of the Law." The power of Nam-myoho-renge-kyo enables us to do this.

For that reason, we don't need to compare ourselves with others. We should simply live in a way that is true to ourselves, based on faith in the Gohonzon.

Please advance in good health and with clear goals, while cultivating positive, harmonious relations with those around you. By conducting yourself in this way, you will naturally become the kind of person others admire, are drawn to, and want to get to know. The Mystic Law enables you to utilize your potential to the fullest. When that happens, you can go anywhere and face anything with a sense of confidence and ease. You'll be able to do what you need to do, unswayed by immediate events and circumstances, and lead a life of deep satisfaction, without regrets. That is the mark of a true victor in life.

From a speech delivered at the 48th Soka Gakkai Headquarters Leaders Meeting, Makiguchi Memorial Hall, Hachioji, Tokyo, April 21, 2005.

4.7 The Power of Our Determination to Change Suffering Into "Peace and Comfort"

Referring to the towering life state of Nichiren Daishonin, who triumphed over relentless onslaughts of difficulty and persecution, President Ikeda discusses the power of our innermost determination, which can transform any kind of difficulty into "peace and comfort."

■ Nichiren Daishonin's life was a series of hardships and persecutions, including being exiled twice. Some of his disciples questioned where any "peace and comfort" was to be found in all this. But he insisted that difficulties are in fact "peace and comfort" (see OTT, 115) and in his writings repeatedly made such statements as: "What fortune is mine!" (WND-1, 402); "How delighted I am!" (Ibid.); "In future lives I will enjoy immense happiness, a thought that gives me great joy" (WND-1, 287); and "How can such joy possibly be described!" (WND-1, 396). He savored a state of life that he could only describe as "How fortunate, how joyful!" (WND-1, 642).

In the light of the Buddhist scriptures, difficulties are inevitable. The important thing is how we transform them, changing poison into medicine, and use them as the driving force for fresh growth and progress.

There is no point in feeling anxious or lamenting each time the harsh winds of adversity blow. If we have a powerful determination to change everything that happens into a strong "tailwind," we can surely open the way forward.

We of the SGI have been able to create a history of tremendous development based on faith that is focused on the present and the future—namely, always looking from the present moment onward and moving forward, ever forward.

Without hardships, there is no true Buddhist practice. Without struggle, there is no genuine happiness. And that would not be real life. There would be no attainment of Buddhahood, either. When we practice Nichiren Buddhism with this understanding, we will never reach an impasse.

The power of one's state of life is indeed wondrous. The power of one's inner determination is limitless. In identical situations or circumstances, people can achieve completely different results and lead completely different lives depending upon their life state and their determination.

Those who have a strong resolve to promote our movement for kosen-rufu will see clear blue skies of good fortune appearing rapidly in their lives, stretching ever further and further, as if the wind were sweeping away every dark cloud.

From a speech delivered ata Nagano Prefecture General Meeting, Nagano Training Center, Karuizawa, Nagano, August 4, 1991.

4.8 Polishing Ourselves Through Adversity

If we practice this Buddhism to become happy, why do we have to overcome hardships? In this section, President Ikeda explains that, just as a diamond is forged through extreme pressure, overcoming great adversity forges us into invincible "champions of life."

■ Why do we have to endure hardships? The purpose of our Buddhist practice is to attain Buddhahood. Buddhahood is the state of absolute happiness. Though we are practicing Nichiren Buddhism to become happy, why then do we have to overcome obstacles? The reason is that we need to undergo the trials of difficulty to forge and strengthen within us the diamond-like and indestructible "self" of Buddhahood.

The diamond is regarded as the king of gemstones. It is the hardest of all minerals, possessing unmatched brilliance. A symbol of purity, its name derives from the Greek word *adamas* meaning "unconquerable" or "invincible."

How are diamonds formed? I'm not a scientist, but it is widely known that diamonds, like graphite, are made of carbon. Deep in the earth, this material is subjected to intense heat and pressure until it is transformed into the crystalline structure of a diamond.

This is similar to how we develop ourselves. Only when subjected to the concentrated pressure of hardships and the fierce heat of great adversity will the core of our lives, our deepest self, be transformed into the diamond-like and indestructible life state of Buddhahood. In other words, it is through experiencing hardships that we acquire the "diamond-like body," or the Buddha body—a brightly shining state of absolute happiness as indestructible as a diamond that cannot be crushed by any amount of suffering or delusion.

A smooth and uneventful kind of Buddhist practice without any difficulties cannot truly help us polish and forge our lives. It is only when we withstand the intense heat and pressure of great hardships that we can shine as "champions of life," sparkling like the most perfect of diamonds.

Such a diamond-like state of life shines with a pure, beautiful, and imperishable light. It is solid and indestructible when buffeted by the turbulent tides of society and the obstacles of corrupt and ill-intentioned forces. We can achieve this state of life through earnestly chanting Nam-myoho-renge-kyo and dedicating ourselves to kosen-rufu. Then our lives will forever be one with the Mystic Law, and we can strive for kosen-rufu with complete freedom throughout eternity. By correctly embracing and upholding the Gohonzon, we can become our greatest possible selves, continuing in this supreme state of Buddhahood in lifetime after lifetime.

Please lead brilliant lives that are diamond-like and indestructible. Indeed, may you all become "diamonds" of happiness that sparkle with the radiance of your beautiful hearts. To do so, please never fear hardships. Don't allow yourselves to be defeated by unfounded criticism. Rather, be grateful for all obstacles, because they help you polish and develop yourselves.

Those who show even stronger conviction in faith and engage even more joyfully in Buddhist practice the greater the hardships they encounter will truly live as diamond-like champions.

Please magnificently adorn this precious life with beautiful faith and beautiful friendship. Live out your days spreading the sublime diamond-like light of life far and wide and demonstrating the truth of the teachings and principles of Nichiren Buddhism.

From a speech delivered at a Funabashi Leaders Meeting, Funabashi Culture Center, Funabashi, Chiba Prefecture, July 13, 1987.

4.9 Winter Always Turns to Spring

Nichiren Daishonin encouraged the lay nun Myoichi with the words, "Winter always turns to spring" (WND-1, 536). In this passage, President Ikeda tells us that life's winters are times for strengthening ourselves in preparation for the arrival of a wonderful spring, and those who embrace the correct teaching of Buddhism will be in harmony with the rhythm of life and the universe and are guaranteed to experience a springtime of victory that shines eternally.

■ Nichiren Daishonin writes, "Winter always turns to spring" (WND-1, 536). Those who believe in the Lotus Sutra may seem to be in winter, he says, but winter will definitely give way to spring.

These words of the Daishonin have enabled countless individuals to find their way forward to a springtime of rebirth, a springtime in life. It is one of our eternal guidelines, and its message, without a doubt, will continue to impart boundless hope to billions of people around the world who are searching for true happiness. Let us then consider the infinite compassion of the Daishonin that is embodied in these words.

He wrote them to encourage the widowed lay nun Myoichi. Her husband had been a person of strong faith. After the Tatsunokuchi Persecution, he was stripped of his estate because of his faith in Nichiren's teachings. Those who are in the right are often persecuted—that is the unfortunate way of our corrupt world, a constant we can observe in every country and every age. While Nichiren was in exile on Sado, Myoichi's husband died, remaining steadfast in faith to the end of his life. He left behind his wife who was elderly and frail, a son who was ill, and a daughter.

Nichiren was very aware of the lay nun's situation. In his letter, he imagined how grieved her husband must have been to leave her and their children behind, worried about what would become of them when he was no longer there, and how he would also have been anxious about the fate of the Daishonin (see WND-1, 535–36).

As I mentioned, Myoichi's husband died while Nichiren was still in exile on Sado, an island of freezing winters from which few exiles returned alive. His heart must have been filled with sorrow and concern for the Daishonin.

Thinking of his courageous disciple who had passed away amid severe hardship, Nichiren writes:

> Perhaps your husband felt that certainly something would happen and this priest [Nichiren] would become highly respected. When I was exiled [to Sado] contrary to his expectations, he must have wondered how the Lotus Sutra and the ten demon daughters[40] could possibly have allowed it to happen. Were he still living, how delighted he would be to see Nichiren pardoned![41] (WND-1, 536)

As this passage and other letters indicate, many of Nichiren's disciples had expected that he would achieve a position of acclaim and honor. In reality, however, his life was filled with endless persecution. He was defamed and ridiculed throughout the land and subjected to unrelenting harassment. Among his followers were some who had expected their own reputations to rise along with his, but when their hopes in this regard were dashed they abandoned their Buddhist practice or joined the ranks of the Daishonin's opponents. They conspired with the authorities and began to maneuver behind the scenes to harm their former teacher and fellow practitioners.

Yet even amid all this, Myoichi's husband remained true and steadfast in his convictions. He must have dreamed of Nichiren's triumphant return and been angered and pained at the mean-spirited betrayal by some of his followers.

The Daishonin knew what was going on in his disciples' minds. He was fully aware of everything. He refused to compromise in the slightest degree with evil and injustice and confronted persecution head-on.

That is why Nichiren writes that Myoichi's deceased husband would surely have been delighted and overjoyed at his safe return from Sado—an outcome that no one at the time had expected. This passage powerfully communicates his wish that his faithful follower, who had stood by him through great hardships, could witness his victory and rejoice along with him.

In the same letter, the Daishonin writes that Myoichi's late husband would also have been glad to see that Nichiren's prediction of a Mongol invasion had come true, affirming the correctness of his assertions. Though foreign invasion, of course, was a tragic event for the country, such a reaction from a disciple was simply a matter of human nature, he points out, "the feelings of ordinary people" (see WND-1, 536).

No doubt upon reading this, the lay nun Myoichi felt she could hear the Daishonin's voice saying, "We are united in our joys and sufferings."

Nichiren's words "winter always turns to spring" are written with regard to the circumstances just described. He is telling her, in effect: "Your husband died in 'winter.' But 'spring' has now arrived. Winter always turns to spring. Live out your life to the fullest. Those who remain true to their convictions are sure to attain Buddhahood. You cannot fail to become happy. Your husband is most certainly watching over you and your family."

In addition, with deep care and compassion, the Daishonin assures Myoichi that he stands ready to look after her children if the time ever arises (see WND-1, 536). Such limitless kindness and warm humanity are the lifeblood of the compassionate Buddhism of Nichiren Daishonin. There is not the slightest trace of authoritarianism. How wonderful!

The words "winter always turns to spring" can also be read as an expression of Nichiren's own conviction and actual proof, having experienced the spring of victory after weathering the bleakest circumstances during his exile on Sado.

He faced persecution after persecution, trials that could not be surmounted without the power of Buddhahood. Ordinarily, someone subject to such ongoing persecution would most likely fall ill, have a nervous breakdown, commit suicide, or end up being killed. Nichiren Daishonin, however, triumphed over every adversity. He survived and lived on. For the sake of all humankind, he transmitted the Buddhism of the Three Great Secret Laws for the eternal future of the Latter Day of the Law. We must be deeply aware of his immense compassion in doing so.

The lay nun Myoichi was no doubt profoundly moved by the Daishonin's message calling on his followers to observe his victory of "winter turning into spring" and to adopt it as a model in their own lives.

We also need to attain our own "spring of happiness"—not only for ourselves but also for the sake of our fellow members who have striven alongside us for many long years. It is important for us to set an example so that those coming after us can look at us, rejoice, and say: "How wonderful! Those who continue practicing Nichiren Buddhism become outstanding people and attain happiness!"

Over the past decade, I have attained a "spring of victory" that no one could have imagined. It is all due to my single-minded commitment for the sake of kosen-rufu and for my fellow members.

Seniors in faith have a responsibility to demonstrate victory for the sake of their fellow members who have been striving valiantly for kosen-rufu. By victory, of course, I do not mean the external trappings of worldly success or superficial honors. True victory exists in realizing the great uncrowned state of having joyfully and confidently fulfilled one's mission in life, as a human being and as a practitioner of Nichiren Buddhism.

Spring is the time when flowers bloom. But in order to bloom, flowers need the cold of winter. What would happen if there was no winter?

In autumn, plants that bloom in spring prepare to enter a period of dormancy, or recharging. They start saving energy for the coming spring. If there is a sudden warm spell during their dormancy in winter and they are awakened, the buds waiting for spring's arrival start to open before they are ready, and when the winter cold returns, they wither and die. To prevent that from happening, plants will not bloom unless they have fully experienced the cold of winter. This is the "wisdom" of plants that enables them to bloom in spring.

Life and Buddhist practice also follow this principle. A winter of adversity is the time to recharge our batteries and temper ourselves for the arrival of a wonderful spring. In life's winters, the eternal and indestructible energy for attaining Buddhahood is stored up, and life force as vast as the universe is forged. This energy, in addition, grows in response to adversity and hardship. And all who practice the correct teaching of Buddhism will without fail experience the coming of spring.

But if, in the difficult times of life's winters, we try to avoid or doubt the realm in which we strengthen our faith, and as a result fail to accumulate enough strength and good fortune, we will never get anywhere, nor will we be able to lead a truly satisfying life. The crucial thing is how we challenge ourselves and how meaningfully we spend our time during life's winters. What matters is how deeply we live with the conviction that spring will definitely arrive. In the realm of nature, the flowering springtime always comes when the time is right. That is the rhythm of life and the universe. But far too many people in the world are still in the midst of winter when they reach the end of their lives. To avoid that fate, we need to align our lives with the rhythm of the universe that calls forth spring. And our Buddhist practice based on faith in the Mystic Law is what enables us to do that.

In that sense, faith in the Mystic Law functions as our wings to eternal happiness. Every time we overcome difficulties, we accumulate good fortune and elevate our state of life. By attaining Buddhahood in this lifetime, we are able to soar serenely through the vast skies of life in a state of supreme happiness and fulfillment throughout eternity. This is the teaching of Buddhism and the rhythm of life.

From a speech delivered at the 28th Headquarters Leaders Meeting, Soka University Central Gymnasium, Hachioji, Tokyo, April 29, 1990.

4.10 The Great Benefit of Buddhist Practice

To encourage his followers, Nichiren offered insight from various perspectives into the meaning of hardship and suffering in life. Writing to the Ikegami brothers, Munenaka and Munenaga, who were being persecuted for their Buddhist faith, Nichiren teaches them the principle of "lessening karmic retribution." Based on the perspective of life spanning the three existences of past, present, and future, this principle teaches that our Buddhist practice has the power to reduce any great karmic suffering we are destined to experience in the future to much lighter suffering in the present. In this excerpt, President Ikeda explains that, in accord with the principle of lessening karmic retribution, we should regard times of suffering and hardships as opportunities for great inner development, using them to grow stronger and more resilient in life.

■ Nichiren Daishonin offered the following encouragement to the Ikegami brothers, Munenaka and Munenaga, who were in the midst of a struggle against serious obstacles, "The blessings gained by practicing the correct teaching [the Mystic Law], however, are so great that by meeting minor sufferings in this life we can change the karma that destines us to suffer terribly in the future" (WND-1, 497).

Through "the blessings gained by practicing the correct teaching"—that is, "the blessings obtained by protecting the Law,"[42] the grave negative effects of karma that we would otherwise have experienced in the future are transformed and received as minor effects in the present. We need to be deeply convinced of this principle, called "lessening karmic retribution."[43] And, to a degree that accords with the depth of our faith, we can experience its reality in our own lives.

For instance, suppose you meet with an accident, but it is very minor and not a disaster that involves many people. This could be an instance of receiving the effects of negative karma in a lessened form. You can probably think of many similar examples.

In this way, we can clearly see the significance of hardships from the perspective of the eternity of life across the three existences of past, present, and future. In other words, by undergoing hardships, we can transform in this lifetime the cycle of negative causes and effects in our lives and magnificently reveal within us the brilliant, vibrant state of Buddhahood.

Nichiren Daishonin discussed these principles of "lessening karmic retribution" and "the blessings obtained by protecting the Law" in terms of his own life in works such as "The Opening of the Eyes" and "Letter from Sado," which he composed while in exile on Sado Island. Though the Buddha of the Latter Day of the Law, he strove as an ordinary person to demonstrate, for the sake of his followers into the eternal future of the Latter Day, the reason why we encounter difficulties. He also taught us the essence of "faith for overcoming hardships." This is a crucial guideline both for our personal lives and for the realm of kosen-rufu.

Three years ago (in October 1985), I was hospitalized for the first time in my life, for ten days. Objectively speaking, I could have collapsed at any moment. After all, I had been working relentlessly for forty years since joining the Soka Gakkai, and nearly thirty years since I had inherited the mantle of our organization's leadership from Mr. Toda.

I had been pushing myself to the limit, even though when I was younger the doctors had said I probably wouldn't live to see the age of thirty. I was constantly on the go. I was always fighting against adversity.

The media made a big fuss about my hospitalization. There were also many unfounded speculations, and some people moved to act against me motivated by self-interest and calculation. But I understood exactly what was happening.

Personally, I felt that my illness was a gift arising from the Buddha's great compassion. I was convinced it was teaching me that the time had come to stand up again on my own and start in earnest on completing my work for kosen-rufu.

Now, I thought, is the time to speak the full truth. Now is the time to offer, from every angle, thoroughgoing guidance for the sake of future generations. I resolved that I must convey the Soka Gakkai's true greatness and its profound significance and spirit.

Until then, I thought I had done my utmost to build a solid organization and teach all that had been necessary. But now, with my illness, I pledged to teach ten or twenty times more and to work ten or twenty times harder. And I began, and continue, to do so.

What I am saying is that you are bound to encounter obstacles and difficulties in life of one degree or another. But please know that they all derive from the Buddha's compassion, aimed at helping you become strong, like tall, sturdy trees.

With that conviction, please forge ahead as champions of faith, overcoming all challenges and opening the way forward in your lives and for kosen-rufu with ever greater strength, resilience, and joy with each obstacle you face.

From a speech delivered at a Nationwide Youth Division Leaders Meeting, Tokyo Ikeda Auditorium, Setagaya, Tokyo, April 29, 1988.

CHAPTER 5

Happiness for Both Ourselves and Others

Introduction to the Chapter:

"If one lights a fire for others, one will brighten one's own way" (WND-2, 1060), writes Nichiren Daishonin, teaching us that working for the happiness of others also makes our own lives shine with happiness.

This chapter focuses on a way of life that is dedicated to the pursuit of happiness for ourselves and for others, which is the purpose of our practice of Nichiren Buddhism.

Buddhism teaches that our lives and our environment are inextricably connected. President Ikeda, therefore, repeatedly stresses that our happiness should not be built upon the misfortune of others, and that we cannot be truly happy while others are suffering. Selfishly seeking personal happiness without concern for others' happiness will not lead to genuine, lasting happiness. At the same time, he notes, thinking only of others without concern for our own well-being is not real happiness, either.

What, then, is the true path to happiness for both ourselves and others?

Nichiren assigned particular importance to the behavior of

Bodhisattva Never Disparaging, whose story is related in the Lotus Sutra. Believing that all living beings possess the Buddha nature, Bodhisattva Never Disparaging showed unwavering respect for everyone he met, even if they reviled or attacked him. By respecting others in this way, he made his own Buddha nature shine brightly.

Faith in Nam-myoho-renge-kyo—the essence of the Lotus Sutra—is the key to unlocking the Buddha nature inherent in all people. Chanting Nam-myoho-renge-kyo and teaching others to do the same leads to happiness for both ourselves and others.

5.1 "'Joy' Means That Oneself and Others Together Experience Joy"

Referring to a passage in The Record of the Orally Transmitted Teachings, *President Ikeda affirms that true joy arises from both ourselves and others becoming happy together. Indicating that faith in the Mystic Law encompasses the wisdom and compassion to achieve that goal, he stresses that our mission as practitioners of Nichiren Buddhism is to create an age in which individual happiness and social prosperity go hand in hand.*

■ Nichiren Daishonin declares: "'Joy' means that oneself and others together experience joy. . . . Both oneself and others together will take joy in their possession of wisdom and compassion" (OTT, 146).

Both ourselves and others matter. Caring only about one's own happiness is selfish. Claiming to care only about the happiness of others is hypocritical. Real "joy" lies in both ourselves and others becoming happy together.

President Toda said: "Becoming happy yourself is no great challenge; it's quite simple. But the essence of Nichiren Buddhism lies in helping others become happy too."[44]

The earlier passage by Nichiren plainly states that true happiness means possessing both wisdom and compassion—in other words, the life state of Buddhahood. If one has wisdom but lacks compassion, one's life will be closed and constricted. Such wisdom, then, is not genuine. To have compassion but lack wisdom or behave foolishly is to be of no help to anyone, including oneself. And compassion that is incapable of helping anyone cannot be said to be genuine.

Only faith in the Mystic Law encompasses both wisdom and compassion. Nichiren clearly states, "Now, when Nichiren and his followers chant Nam-myoho-renge-kyo, they are expressing joy in the fact that they will inevitably become Buddhas eternally endowed with the three bodies"[45] (OTT, 146). This in itself is "the greatest of all joys" (OTT, 212).

President Toda maintained that "individual happiness and social prosperity must go hand in hand." The individual happiness referred to here is not self-centered; rather, it means cultivating true humanity—developing into a person who possesses wisdom and compassion and helping others do the same.

The Lotus Sutra (Nam-myoho-renge-kyo) has the power to actualize both individual happiness and social prosperity.

Adapted from the dialogue The Wisdom of the Lotus Sutra, *vol. 5, published in Japanese in September 1999.*

5.2 The Bodhisattva Way Enables Us to Benefit Both Ourselves and Others

President Ikeda speaks of the bodhisattva way, the path through which our lives are invigorated and expanded by helping others invigorate and expand their lives, in a mutually supportive process of benefiting ourselves and others.

There are countless people in the world whose hearts have been wounded in some way. We need to extend a healing hand to such individuals. Through such efforts, we in fact heal ourselves.

When beset by some misfortune, people tend to think that no one could possibly be as unhappy or unlucky as they are. They feel sorry for themselves and become blind to everything but their own situation. They wallow in their suffering, feeling dissatisfied and hopeless, which only saps their life force further.

At such times, what gives someone the strength to go on living? It seems to me that it is human bonds—the desire to live for the sake of others. As long as we are wrapped up in ourselves, there is no happiness. When we courageously take action for others, the wellspring of our own life is replenished.

When we look after and care for others—that is, help others draw forth their life force—our own life force increases. When we help people expand their state of life, our state of life also expands. That is the wonderful thing about the bodhisattva way. The practice for benefiting others is one and the same with the practice for benefiting ourselves.

To only speak of benefiting others leads to arrogance. It conveys a sense of self-righteousness, as if we are somehow doing others a favor by "saving" them. Only when we recognize that our efforts on others' behalf are also for our own sake will we be filled with humble appreciation for being able to develop our lives.

Our lives and the lives of others are ultimately inseparable. It is vital, therefore, that we follow the bodhisattva way.

Adapted from the dialogue The Wisdom of the Lotus Sutra, *vol. 4, published in Japanese in December 1998.*

5.3 The Path of Mutual Respect and Growth

The aim of Buddhism is the pursuit of happiness. President Ikeda speaks of the importance of a life committed to mutual growth and development, in which we respect and value our fellow seekers of happiness as we humbly and tirelessly strive for that shared goal.

■ Buddhism is the pursuit of happiness. The purpose of faith is to become happy; we carry out Buddhist practice for the sake of our own happiness.

Aniruddha, one of Shakyamuni's ten major disciples, known as the foremost in divine insight, once dozed off while Shakyamuni was preaching. Deeply reflecting on his behavior, he vowed never to sleep again. As a result of his unremitting practice, he eventually went blind. Later, though, he is said to have opened his mind's eye and thereby gained extraordinary powers of discernment.

One day, Aniruddha attempted to mend a tear in his robe. But because he couldn't see, he was unable to thread the sewing needle. In his frustration, he muttered, "Is there no one who will thread this needle for me and so gain good fortune [from helping a practitioner of Buddhism]?"

Someone approached him and said, "Allow me to accumulate good fortune."

Aniruddha was stunned. For it was unmistakably the voice of Shakyamuni.

"I couldn't possibly trouble you," he protested, adding: "Surely one such as yourself, World-Honored One, does not need to gain any benefit."

"On the contrary, Aniruddha," Shakyamuni responded, "there is no greater seeker of happiness in the world than myself."[46]

Shakyamuni went on to teach Aniruddha, who was still not convinced by his words, that there are things that one must continue to pursue eternally. For instance, in seeking truth, there is never an end, a point where we can say, "This will do." Similarly, in our efforts to lead others to enlightenment, there is no limit at which we can say, "I have done enough." The same goes for our practice to develop and perfect ourselves.

The pursuit of happiness also has no bounds. Shakyamuni told Aniruddha: "Of all the powers in the world, and in the realms of heaven or human beings, the power of good fortune is foremost. The Buddha way, too, is attained through the power of good fortune."[47]

Shakyamuni's words "There is no greater seeker of happiness in the world than myself" have important meaning.

Buddhism is not about turning one's back on life or escaping reality, or acting as if one has already attained enlightenment and risen above considerations of happiness and unhappiness. In particular, thinking oneself alone to be special has nothing to do with Buddhism.

Rather, genuine practitioners of Buddhism are those who, as humble seekers of happiness, earnestly pursue their Buddhist practice together with and in the same way as everyone else. They take action with courage and joy, more determined than anyone to never pass up an opportunity to accumulate good fortune. Such people never arrogantly think, "This is good enough," but continue to exert themselves out of a desire to gain still more fortune and benefit and to develop a state of eternal happiness. The spirit of Buddhism pulses in this resolve to keep improving and challenging oneself without end.

Shakyamuni's simple offer to thread Aniruddha's needle conveys his infinitely profound spirit and attitude toward life. His conduct is a natural expression of his egalitarian philosophy to regard his fellow practitioners as equals.

In *The Record of the Orally Transmitted Teachings,* Nichiren states, "It is like the situation when one faces a mirror and makes a bow of obeisance: the image in the mirror likewise makes a bow of obeisance to oneself" (OTT, 165).

Believing in others' Buddha nature, we respect and treasure them from the bottom of our hearts. When we treat others in this manner, the Buddha nature within them responds, on a fundamental level, with respect toward us in return.

Broadly speaking, when we interact with others with true sincerity, more often than not they will come to respect and value us as well. And this is all the more so when our actions are based on prayer—chanting Nam-myoho-renge-kyo.

Conversely, denigrating others only leads to being denigrated oneself. And those whose lives are tainted by feelings of hate toward others will come to be reviled by others in turn.

Let us open the path to mutual respect and harmonious coexistence so as to bring an end to this vicious circle that has long been part of human destiny.

From a speech delivered at a European Representatives Conference, Frankfurt, Germany, June 11, 1992.

5.4 Treasuring the Present Moment and the People Right in Front of Us

Referring to a story by the Russian author Leo Tolstoy, President Ikeda highlights the importance of the present moment and the people we are connected to right now, and emphasizes that we gain trust through valuing those around us.

■ Tolstoy wrote many very accessible stories and folk tales. He composed them for ordinary people who lived off the land, and for the young boys and girls who would inherit the future.

Today, I would like to share with you one of those stories, titled "Three Questions."

The story concerns an emperor who, in directing the affairs of state, finds himself wondering about three questions.

The first question is: What is the best time to do each thing?

The second question is: Who are the most important people to work with?

The third question is: What is the most important thing to do at all times?

The emperor very much wants to know the answers to these questions, because he is sure that if he has the answers, he could succeed in everything he does. He makes it known throughout the land that he will richly reward anyone who can tell him the right answers to these questions. Many learned people come to see him, and they offer many answers. But the emperor is not convinced by any of them.

The learned are not necessarily wise.

I will leave out the details of the story, but in the end the emperor gains the true answers to his questions from a hermit who lives among the people.

This wise man replies that the most important time is now, this very moment; the most important person is the one in front of you right now; and the most important task is doing good to others, caring about others' happiness.

This moment, this instant is important, not some unknown time in the future. Today, this very day, is what matters. We must put our entire beings into the present—for future victory is contained in this moment.

Likewise, we do not need to look for special people in some far-off place. People are not made important simply by virtue of their power, learning, fame, or riches. The most important people are those in our immediate environment right now. They are the people we must value. Wise individuals consider the unique characteristics of those around them and make it possible for them to bring out their full potential. This is also the way to win the trust and respect of everyone.

Whenever I travel abroad, I always endeavor to sincerely greet and connect with the very first people I meet after getting off the plane—and then do the same with all those I meet thereafter. This is how my efforts to foster friendship start.

It is not important whether you are unknown or unremarkable in the world's eyes. What matters is that you know you have done your best, in a way that is true to yourself, for the sake of others, for your friends, and for people in society at large. Those who can declare that with confidence are champions of the human spirit, champions of life.

From a speech delivered at an SGI Asian Commemorative General Meeting, Hong Kong Culture Centre, Hong Kong, May 16, 1993.

5.5 We Are Enriched by Helping Others

Nichiren Buddhism is the path for attaining happiness for ourselves and others, for enabling everyone to be victors in life. Doing our utmost to support and encourage others toward that goal enriches us and becomes a precious treasure within our own lives.

■ While sowing the seeds of happiness in the life of one person after another may seem like a long, roundabout process, it is actually the most fundamental groundwork for changing our planet as a whole.

Although it takes a long time for a tree to grow from a tiny seed, when it does grow big and tall, it will bear abundant flowers and fruit, and people will find rest in its cool shade. Each of us must strive to become such a tall tree.

Nichiren Buddhism is the path for attaining happiness for ourselves and others. It advocates neither sacrificing others nor sacrificing ourselves. It may be noble to sacrifice oneself for others, but it is not something we can expect of everyone. If we did, it would lead to a very unnatural situation.

Our real aim is the happiness of both ourselves and others. We need a path that empowers everyone to be a victor in life. That means, while we strive for others' happiness, we do so with a deep sense of appreciation for them—"All of my struggles to help him have made me into a much better person. How wonderful!" "The efforts I made to support her have made me so much stronger. How grateful I am!" The fact is, the harder we strive for kosen-rufu, the greater the good fortune and wisdom we will acquire. SGI activities benefit others and ourselves at the same time.

For example, you meet and talk with someone, you chant for

someone's happiness, or you write a postcard or letter to someone. Perhaps someone you arranged to meet didn't show up, but you continue to stay in touch and meet with them again and again. These may seem like small things, and you may sometimes feel you're not getting anywhere. But when you look back later, you'll see that none of your efforts were wasted. You'll see that going to meet others and encouraging them has made you a stronger, bigger person. You'll discover that chanting for a friend's happiness has enriched your own life enormously. The more time passes—ten years, twenty years on—the more you'll see that your every action has become a precious treasure for you.

And the day will come when those you have reached out to will show their appreciation. Someday they will happily tell others that you helped them stand up in faith or become the people they are today.

Your aim is to play that role in the lives of as many people as you can. There is no greater treasure in life than this.

Adapted from the dialogue Discussions on Youth, *published in Japanese in September 2000.*

5.6 The Bodhisattva Practice of Respecting All People

President Ikeda teaches that practicing the bodhisattva way based on a spirit of compassion—deeply respecting the Buddha nature inherent in all people and drawing forth that ultimate dignity from our own lives and those of others—is the great path to happiness for both ourselves and others.

■ Our happiness does not exist apart from the happiness of others. The Buddhist's foundation for action is the spirit of compassion. Compassion has two aspects—relieving suffering and providing ease. It seeks to eliminate people's anxieties and fears and impart joy, reassurance, and hope.

As a Buddhist—and, indeed, as a human being—taking action for people's happiness is only natural. But sometimes the simplest things can be the most difficult. The essence of the teachings of Buddhism is simple: treasure each person. A Buddha is one who strives and works tirelessly for the happiness of every single individual.

In Buddhism, those whose actions are based on the spirit of benefiting others, or altruism, are called bodhisattvas. Numerous bodhisattvas appear in the Buddhist scriptures—for instance, Manjushri, Universal Worthy, Maitreya, Perceiver of the World's Sounds, and Medicine King, to name but a few. Each of these bodhisattvas uses their unique qualities to serve living beings, working to protect and save them from various forms of suffering and misfortune. For example, Manjushri does so with wisdom, Universal Worthy with learning, and Maitreya with compassion. Perceiver of the World's Sounds relieves the sufferings of living beings through his power to perceive what is taking place in the world. Medicine King, as his name indicates, cures illnesses with beneficial medicines.

Of all the many bodhisattvas, Nichiren focuses on Bodhisattva Never Disparaging in the Lotus Sutra as a model for practice. As the bodhisattva's name indicates, he never disparages anyone, showing the highest respect for all.

In the Lotus Sutra, Bodhisattva Never Disparaging greets people respectfully, saying: "I have profound reverence for you, I would never dare treat you with disparagement or arrogance. Why? Because you will all practice the bodhisattva way and will then be able to attain Buddhahood" (LSOC, 308). This is a distillation of the Lotus Sutra's spirit of respect for the dignity of all human beings. As described in the sutra, Bodhisattva Never Disparaging presses his hands together in reverence and bows to all whom he meets.

Nichiren identifies the actions of Bodhisattva Never Disparaging as the essence of the practice of Buddhism, writing, "The heart of the Buddha's lifetime of teachings is the Lotus Sutra, and the heart of the practice of the Lotus Sutra is found in the '[Bodhisattva] Never Disparaging' chapter" (WND-1, 851–52).

The behavior of Bodhisattva Never Disparaging is based on his conviction that all living beings are noble because they possess the Buddha nature. By revealing their Buddha nature—the universal nobility or dignity inherent within them—any and every individual can open the way to an unparalleled life. Advancing on this path together with others is the practice of the bodhisattva way.

Adapted from the dialogue A Dialogue on Human Rights in the Twenty-first Century,[48] *published in Japanese in February 1995.*

5.7 Accumulating Treasures of the Heart and Helping Others Do the Same

Stressing that our bodhisattva practice for the happiness of others will become an eternal record of achievement that magnificently adorns our lives, President Ikeda here speaks of a life in which we accumulate treasures of the heart and help others do the same.

■ By helping others become happy, we, too, become happy. This is also a tenet of psychology. How can those who have lost the will to live under the weight of inconsolable suffering or deep emotional wounds get back on their feet? All too often, the more they dwell on their problem, the more depressed and discouraged they become. But by going to support and help someone else who is also suffering, they can regain the will to live. Taking action out of concern for others enables them to heal themselves.

There are many people in the world who feel that working for others' welfare is not worth the effort. Some even view the mere mention of charity and compassion with derision. Such arrogant disregard for others causes untold suffering in society.

An American missionary supposedly once asked Mahatma Gandhi: "What religion do you practice and what form do you think religion will take in India in the future?" Two sick people happened to be resting in the room. Pointing in their direction, Gandhi replied simply: "My religion is serving and working for the people. I am not preoccupied with the future."[49]

For Gandhi, politics and government were also a matter of service and, as Rabindranath Tagore said, of helping "the most destitute."[50]

It's all about action. In essence, altruistic bodhisattva practice is the very heart of religion, of Buddhism, and also of humane government and education.

We have a tremendous mission. Nichiren writes: "More valuable than treasures in a storehouse are the treasures of the body, and the treasures of the heart are the most valuable of all" (WND-1, 851). To focus only on the "treasures of the storehouse"—finances or the economy—will not improve the economic situation. Things may improve for a while, but this will ultimately not contribute to the welfare of society. It is people, it is the heart, that matter most. The heart determines everything. When we possess the "treasures of the heart," when our lives overflow with good fortune and wisdom, we will naturally be endowed with abundant "treasures of the body" and "treasures of the storehouse."

What is left at the end of our lives? It is our memories, the memories that we have engraved in our hearts and minds.

I met the Russian novelist Mikhail Sholokhov when I visited Moscow in 1974. He told me: "When one lives to an old age, the most painful experiences in life become difficult to recall. The older one grows, the colors of the events in one's life fade and everything from the happiest times to the saddest starts to pass away." After pausing for a moment, he continued with a smile: "When you turn seventy, Mr. Ikeda, you will know that what I am saying is the truth." His words are profound, indeed.

Everything passes. Both the soaring joys and crushing sorrows fade away and seem but like a dream. But the memory of having lived one's life to the fullest never disappears. The memories of having worked wholeheartedly for kosen-rufu, in particular, are eternal.

Surely all that remains and adorns our lives in the end is what we have done or contributed to the world in our lifetime in terms of how many people we have helped become happy, how many people appreciate us for having helped them change their lives for the better.

Nichiren Daishonin writes, "Single-mindedly chant Nam-myoho-renge-kyo and urge others to do the same; that will remain as the only memory of your present life in this human world" (WND-1, 64).

Adapted from the dialogue The Wisdom of the Lotus Sutra, *vol. 5, published in Japanese in September 1999.*

5.8 The Ultimate Way of Benefiting Others Is Sharing the Mystic Law

Stating that Nam-myoho-renge-kyo is the key to unlocking the Buddha nature that all living beings possess, President Ikeda explains that sharing and practicing the Mystic Law with others is the ultimate form of happiness for ourselves and others as taught in Nichiren Buddhism.

■ The reality of life is that people usually cannot even help themselves, much less make their own families happy.

Many political leaders and celebrities pretend to be caring and altruistic, but how many are actually dedicating their lives to the welfare of others?

Our members in the early days of our movement were virtually all poor. Most had no particular social status or higher education. But they possessed a lofty spirit. They were determined to help everyone they encountered become happy. They burned with a sense of great mission as trailblazers for humanity.

There is no nobler way of life than to be committed to helping others, to empowering them to become happy.

I will never forget the words of one of the members who pioneered the movement for kosen-rufu in Peru: "Other than my blood and my bones, what sustained me in this life was just my wish for the happiness of the people of Peru." Those were his last words.

My mentor, Josei Toda, said: "You can give food to the hungry and money to those in need, but you cannot distribute those things equally to all who are wanting. There is a limit to material aid. And the recipients may be glad, but they may also become dependent upon you and think they can continue to receive this support without any effort on their part. The greatest offering one can make is the offering of Buddhism. This allows people to gain fresh life force, enabling them to do their work and to become healthy again. This inner strength, like water welling up from the earth, is limitless."

This is, indeed, the supreme path of benefiting others.

Adapted from the dialogue Discussions on Youth
published in Japanese in September 2000.

CHAPTER 6

Facing the All-Important Questions of Life and Death

Introduction to the Chapter:

What is the purpose of life? What is a truly meaningful existence? What happens after we die? What is death? Nichiren Daishonin urges us to "first of all learn about death, and then about other things" (WND-2, 759), his message being that only by directly facing the inescapable question of death can we build a truly happy life.

The Lotus Sutra, the essence of Buddhism, teaches that our lives are not limited to this present existence but continue eternally. Based on this view of life expressed in the Lotus Sutra, Nichiren Daishonin stresses that a life united with the Mystic Law will forever travel on the path of Buddhahood, transcending the sufferings of birth and death.

President Ikeda expresses this essential message of Nichiren Buddhism in contemporary terms, introducing a magnificent view of existence characterized by joy in both life and death. He describes the way to lead a life of the greatest possible value in this world—in other words, the way to attain Buddhahood in this lifetime.

In an address he gave at Harvard University, President Ikeda shares his insight into these issues: "A central challenge for the coming century will be to establish a culture based on an understanding of the relationship of life and death and of life's essential eternity. Such an attitude does not disown death, but directly confronts and correctly positions it within the larger context of life."[51] *(A selected excerpt from this address appears after section 6.5.)*

6.1 The Path to Absolute Happiness

President Ikeda reaffirms that to overcome the sufferings of birth, aging, sickness, and death and establish a state of eternal happiness, it is crucial to realize Buddhahood in this present lifetime. Toward that end, he stresses the importance of advancing with perseverance, never straying from the path for attaining Buddhahood.

■ Why do we practice Nichiren Buddhism? So that we may live the most wonderful lives. So that we may serenely overcome the four sufferings of birth, aging, sickness, and death that are an inescapable part of the human condition.

The first of the four sufferings is birth. Having been born, we must live out our lives. It is important that we strive to live on tenaciously to the very end, no matter what happens.

Our Buddhist practice based on the Mystic Law gives us the powerful life force to live each day with strength and confidence, surmounting all kinds of problems and hardships. Why are we born? A life lived without meaning, without knowing the answer to that question, is shallow and empty. To just live, eat, and die without any real sense of purpose surely constitutes a base, animal-like existence.

On the other hand, to do, create, or contribute something that benefits others, society, and also ourselves, and to dedicate ourselves as long as we live to that challenge—that is a life of true satisfaction, a life of value, a life of the loftiest humanity. Our Buddhist practice based on the Mystic Law, moreover, is the driving force that enables us to create the greatest possible value for ourselves and for others.

Aging is the second of the four sufferings. Life passes by in a flash. In the blink of an eye, we are old. Our physical strength wanes, and things start to go wrong with our bodies. Our practice of Nichiren Buddhism enables us to make our old age a time of great richness, like a golden autumn harvest, instead of a time of sad and lonely decline. The setting sun bathes the earth and sky in a magnificent glow. We practice Nichiren Buddhism so we can enjoy just such a vibrant, glowing old age, without regrets.

The third of the four sufferings is sickness. We are mortal beings. All of us experience illness in one form or another. The power of the Mystic Law enables us to bring forth the strength to overcome the suffering of sickness. Nichiren Daishonin writes: "Nam-myoho-renge-kyo is like the roar of a lion. What sickness can therefore be an obstacle?" (WND-1, 412).

Though we may fall ill or experience some other trying situation, if we are devoting ourselves to the realization of kosen-rufu, Nichiren Daishonin will protect us, as will all Buddhas and bodhisattvas and the heavenly deities—the protective functions of the universe.

The Daishonin promises:

> A woman who takes this efficacious medicine [of Myoho-renge-kyo] will be surrounded and protected by these four great bodhisattvas [the leaders of the Bodhisattvas of the Earth] at all times. When she rises to her feet, so too will

> the bodhisattvas, and when she walks along the road, they will also do the same. She and they will be as inseparable as a body and its shadow, as fish and water, as a voice and its echo, or as the moon and its light. (WND-1, 415)

As this passage indicates, those who embrace faith in the Mystic Law will definitely be protected—not only in this lifetime but throughout eternity.

Death is the last of the four sufferings. Death is uncompromising; we must all face it one day.

When that moment comes, those who travel on the path of the Mystic Law will make their way serenely to the pure land of Eagle Peak aboard the "great white ox cart"[52] described in the Lotus Sutra. Their lives will merge with the world of Buddhahood of the universe. The Lotus Sutra describes the "great white ox cart" as being immense in every dimension and adorned with gold, silver, and countless precious gems.[53]

If we attain the state of Buddhahood in this existence, that state will forever pervade our lives. In lifetime after lifetime, we will enjoy lives blessed with health, wealth, intellect, favorable circumstances, and good fortune. We will possess our own unique mission and be born in a form suitable to fulfilling that mission. This state of life is everlasting; it can never be destroyed.

It is precisely so that you may enjoy such eternal happiness that I continually urge you to apply yourself to your Buddhist practice and firmly consolidate the state of Buddhahood in your life in this existence. This is not just a matter of personal sentiment. It is the teaching of Nichiren Daishonin.

It's crucial, therefore, that we do not move off the path leading to Buddhahood, but that we keep pressing ever forward with patience and persistence along the path of kosen-rufu and Buddhist practice.

There may well be times when we feel disinclined to do something, or when we would like to take a break. This is only natural, since we are ordinary beings. But what matters is that we stay on course, that we continue forging ahead patiently on the path to Buddhahood while encouraging one another along the way.

If a plane flies off course or a car veers carelessly off the road, it can easily have an accident or fail to reach its destination. Similarly, if our lives go off course, we, too, can crash, plunging into misfortune and misery. Though it may not be visible to the eye, there is a path or course in life. A path leading to absolute happiness exists without a doubt—and that is the path of the Mystic Law.

If we continue on this path without abandoning our Buddhist practice, we will definitely come to savor a life of complete fulfillment, both materially and spiritually.

From a speech delivered at a meeting with representatives of the New York Joint Territories, New York Culture Center, New York, June 15, 1996.

6.2 Death Gives Greater Meaning to Life

How should we regard death? President Ikeda explains that rather than ignoring or denying death, we need to correctly perceive the true nature of existence, the most important and fundamental question in life, and realize that an awareness of the profound implications of death actually affords us the opportunity to lead more meaningful lives.

■ We all know that we will die someday. But we cling to that idea of "someday," expecting it to be far off in the future. Young people naturally try to brush aside the thought of death, but this is even true of older people, and perhaps increasingly so as we age.

But the reality of life is that it may come to an end at any moment. The possibility of death is always with us—be it from an earthquake, an accident, or a sudden illness. We simply choose to forget this.

As someone once noted: "Death does not lie in wait before us; it creeps up on us from behind."

As we keep procrastinating, telling ourselves, "I'll challenge myself harder someday" or "I'll make greater efforts after I finish doing this," our lives slip by and, before we know it, we are facing death without having achieved anything, without having accumulated any really profound inner treasures of life. Many people live their lives this way. When the final moment comes, it's too late for regrets.

Upon reflection, whether death awaits in three days, three years, or three decades, the reality is essentially the same. That's why it is so important to live fully right now, so that we will have no regret if we die at any moment.

From the perspective of eternity, even a century is just an instant. It is genuinely true, as the Daishonin says, that "now is the last moment of one's life" (WND-1, 216). President Toda also said, "In truth, we practice Buddhism for the time of our death."

Nothing is more certain than death. That's why it is vital to immediately set ourselves to the task of accumulating the treasures of the heart that will endure for eternity. Yet the great majority of people put off this most crucial of all tasks or leave it for some future time.

There is nothing as important as what Buddhism calls the "one great matter of life and death." Compared to this crucial matter, everything else is minor—a fact that becomes abundantly clear at the moment of death.

Someone who has been at the bedside of many at their last

moments has said: "In their final days, it seems that people often recall their lives as if gazing over a vast panorama. What appears to stand out are not things such as having led a company or done well in business, but rather how they have lived their lives, whom they have loved, whom they've been kind to, whom they've hurt. All of their deepest emotions—the feeling of having been true to their beliefs and lived a fulfilled life, or painful regrets at having betrayed others—rush upon them as they approach death."

An awareness of death gives greater meaning to our lives. Awakening to death's reality prompts us to seek the eternal and motivates us to make the most of each moment.

What if there were no death? Life would just go on and on and probably become painfully dull.

Death makes us treasure the present. Modern civilization is said to ignore or deny death. It is no coincidence that it is also a civilization characterized by the unfettered pursuit of desires. A society or civilization, just like an individual, that tries to avoid the fundamental question of life and death, will fall into spiritual decline as it fails to look beyond living for the moment.

Adapted from the dialogue The Wisdom of the Lotus Sutra, *vol. 4, published in Japanese in December 1998.*

6.3 The Buddhist View of Life That Transcends the Suffering of Death

Shakyamuni Buddha achieved an awareness of the eternity of life by directly confronting the fundamental human suffering of death. While exploring the nature of Shakyamuni's enlightenment, President Ikeda discusses the essence of the Buddhist view of life and death.

■ All living things have an instinctual fear of death. Human beings in particular are afflicted by an indescribable terror when they contemplate what sort of world may await them after departing from the realm of the living.

With tremendous courage, Shakyamuni overcame this primal human instinct to fear death, to refuse to countenance or contemplate its reality, and accepted the suffering that is the true nature of human existence. Then, based on that courageous stance, he deeply pondered the essence of life and death.

Buddhism teaches the eternity of life, but not as a simplistic response to people's cherished hopes for immortality. The Buddhist teachings of the impermanence of all phenomena and the four noble truths (clarifying the causes and the resolution of human suffering)[54] directly expose the reality of the suffering inherent in life, a reality that people try to avoid. Shakyamuni did not seek to whitewash the reality of existence by offering some consoling myth or fiction; he looked at it directly, with cool objectivity. All things that are born will die. He affirmed this as the underlying truth of existence.

Why do we die? Are life and death completely separate from one another? Or are they closely interrelated? Is there a continuity underlying life itself? Reflecting on his own life, Shakyamuni sought the answers to those questions with courage, tenacity, and objectivity. And the truth to which he became enlightened is that life is eternal.

Human existence includes both life and death. It flows on eternally, with a powerful force, repeating a cycle of alternating manifest and latent phases. Shakyamuni saw this in the flow of his own life.

His is not a philosophy of the immortality of the soul, arising from a dogged attachment to life, but a solid affirmation of the eternity of life based on a recognition of the law of cause and effect unfolding within each individual life.

The significance of death in such a view of life's eternity is that death exists for the sake of life. It is akin to sleep, which provides us with the rest we need to awaken once again. Death is an "expedient means" for life. Death's purpose is to make life shine brighter, while life is the innate activity of existence. Life and death are not in opposition to one another; death exists for the sake of life. This is the meaning of the Lotus Sutra teaching of "entering nirvana as an expedient means" (see LSOC, 271).[55]

The essential message of Buddhism is not pessimistic or negative; nor is it unfounded optimism. Buddhism looks directly at the suffering of life and offers a philosophy for living with joy by actively engaging with reality rather than trying to escape from it. There is no true joy to be had in fleeing from suffering. An indestructible, everlasting, and inexhaustible joy is only achieved by accurately seeing the true reality of the suffering we would like to escape and courageously rising to its challenge and overcoming it.

Adapted from Dialogue on Life, *vol. 3,*[56]
published in Japanese in March 1974.

6.4 The Oneness of Life and Death

What is the Buddhist view of life and death? Based on the teachings of the Lotus Sutra, President Ikeda explains that our existence is eternal, manifesting as life and then becoming latent again as death, in an infinite continuum.

■ Birth and death are different aspects of life. In other words, life manifests solely through the cycle of birth and death.

In the eyes of ordinary mortals, life begins with birth and ends with death. But the insight of Buddhism sees through this limitation and perceives the essence of life as a whole, manifesting actively as birth or existence and persisting in dormant form as death. From that perspective, how does Buddhism view these two aspects of birth and death?

"Life Span," the sixteenth chapter of the Lotus Sutra speaks of "ebbing" and "flowing" (see LSOC, 267). "Ebbing" refers to death and "flowing" to life. Based on the standpoint of the eternity of life, the "Life Span" chapter states that life itself does not disappear and emerge, does not undergo birth or death. In *The Record of the Orally Transmitted Teachings*, Nichiren Daishonin reveals an even more profound view of life as the "originally inherent nature of birth and death" (OTT, 127).[57]

According to this principle, living is the state in which our life is actively manifested, and death is the state when it returns to a latent or potential state. These phases of birth and death continue eternally. That is the true nature of life itself.

The supreme teaching of Buddhism that views living as an active state and death as a latent state offers a profound and magnificent view of the eternity of life.

In addition, it teaches the oneness of life and death. Life is activated by a wondrous, underlying power. When life in its latent state comes into contact with the right causes and conditions, it becomes manifest and takes shape as a dynamic living being with a rich individuality. Eventually, that life quietly ebbs and moves toward death. But as it shifts into its potential, dormant phase, it stores a new energy, awaiting the next new phase of life.

Life is an explosion and burning of the stored up energy that had been in a resting state. Eventually that life brings its story to a close and it drifts back into death. It merges with the universe, is recharged by the power of the life of the universe as a whole, and awaits its next emergence into active life.

This is the nature of life and death inherent in all things, and

Nam-myoho-renge-kyo is the foundation of this intrinsic rhythm of the universe.

Adapted from a lecture on Nichiren Daishonin's writing "The Heritage of the Ultimate Law of Life," published in the April 1997 Seikyo Shimbun.

6.5 Joy in Both Life and Death

President Ikeda spoke at Harvard University on two occasions, in 1991 and 1993. In this excerpt, referring to his 1993 speech "Mahayana Buddhism and Twenty-First-Century Civilization," he stresses that those who dedicate their lives to kosen-rufu and establish a state of absolute happiness can forever travel along a path in which both life and death are filled with joy.

■ On two occasions, I was invited to speak at Harvard University, one of the most prestigious institutions of higher learning in the United States. In my second speech, I addressed the Buddhist view of life and death, in which we can experience joy in both life and death.

Dr. Harvey Cox, then chair of the Harvard Divinity School's Department of Applied Theology, commented that I had presented my audience with a completely new perspective on death.

Death is not the end of everything. Birth and death are both aspects of the eternity of life. The cycle of birth and death grounded in the Mystic Law is a drama unfolding on a great stage of life existing eternally. By striving for kosen-rufu, we can firmly establish a state of absolute happiness in this existence. People who achieve that can advance along the path of joy in both life and death.

This planet Earth is not the only place one can be born. In this vast universe, many scientists believe, there are innumerable planets where life exists. The Lotus Sutra presents a grand and expansive view of the universe, teaching that the number of realms in which living beings reside is infinite—a view that is widely supported by contemporary astronomy. There may be some planets where all the inhabitants are good and virtuous, and others, like our Earth, where there are also many who are selfish and devious. There may also be planets where everyone lives happily, in fine health, enjoying long lives, and listening to beautiful music from morning to night.

When the functions of our hearts and minds and the functions of the universe are in sync, we can be born wherever we wish, and in any form we desire. The Lotus Sutra speaks of "freely choosing where one will be born" (see LSOC, 202). This is the essence of Buddhism.

President Toda often likened death to sleep. Just as we awake refreshed and energized after a good night's sleep, those who pass away having chanted Nam-myoho-renge-kyo throughout their lives will, after a period of rest, be reborn to once again join the ranks of those striving for kosen-rufu, he used to say.

Nichiren Daishonin repeatedly offers guidance about the moment of death in his writings. For example:

> How can we possibly hold back our tears at the inexpressible joy of knowing that [at the moment of death] not just one or two, not just one hundred or two hundred, but as many as a thousand Buddhas will come to greet us with open arms! (WND-1, 216–17)

* * * *

> Without fail, I will be with you at the time of your death and guide you from this life to the next. (WND-1, 965)

* * * *

> When he was alive, he was a Buddha in life, and now he is a Buddha in death. He is a Buddha in both life and death. This is what is meant by that most important doctrine called attaining Buddhahood in one's present form. (WND-1, 456)

A belief in the eternity of life has been shared by many of the world's great writers and thinkers. Their view of life has much in common with the perspective of Buddhism.

Leo Tolstoy (1828–1910) was one such individual. In 1907, when he was seventy-nine, a few years before he passed away, Tolstoy wrote, "Living is joyous, and death, too, is joyous."[58] These words express the unshakable state of mind that Tolstoy had reached after a life of great vicissitudes.

The eminent British historian Arnold J. Toynbee was also deeply impressed by the Buddhist view of life.

We have faith in, are practicing, and are sharing the supreme teaching of Buddhism, eagerly sought by the world's leading thinkers. There is no life more wonderful.

From a speech delivered at a joint training session, Nagano, August 19, 2005.

For further reference

It was the Greek philosopher Heraclitus who declared that all things are in a state of flux and that change is the essential nature of reality. Indeed, everything, whether it lies in the realm of natural phenomena or of human affairs, changes continuously. Nothing maintains exactly the same state for even the briefest instant; the most solid-seeming rocks and minerals are subject to the erosive effects of time. But during this century of war and revolution, normal change and flux seem to have been accelerated and magnified. We have seen the most extraordinary panorama of social transformations.

The Buddhist term for the ephemeral aspect of reality is "the transience of all phenomena" (*shogyo mujo* in Japanese). In the Buddhist cosmology, this concept is described as the repeated cycles of formation, continuance, decline, and disintegration through which all systems must pass.

During our lives as human beings, we experience transience as the four sufferings: the suffering of birth (and of day-to-day existence), that of illness, of aging, and finally, of death. No human being is exempt from these sources of pain. It was, in fact, human distress, in particular the problem of death, that spawned the formation of religious and philosophical systems.

It is said that Shakyamuni was inspired to seek the truth by his accidental encounters with many sorrows at the gates of the palace in which he was raised. Plato stated that true philosophers are always engaged in the practice of dying, while Nichiren, founder of the school of Buddhism followed by members of Soka Gakkai International, admonishes us to "first of all learn about death, and then about other things" (WND-2, 759).

Death weighs heavily on the human heart as an inescapable reminder of the finite nature of our existence. However seemingly limitless the wealth or power we might attain, the reality of our eventual demise cannot be avoided. From ancient times, humanity has sought to conquer the fear and apprehension surrounding death by finding ways to partake of the eternal. Through this quest, people have learned to overcome control by instinctual modes of survival and have developed the characteristics that we recognize as uniquely human. In that perspective, we can see why the history of religion coincides with the history of humankind.

Modern civilization has attempted to ignore death. We have diverted our gaze from this most fundamental of concerns as we try to drive death into the shadows. For many people living today, death is the mere absence of life; it is blankness; it is the void. Life is identified with all that is good: with being, rationality, and light. In contrast, death is perceived as evil, as nothingness, and as the dark and irrational. Only the negative perception of death prevails.

We cannot, however, ignore death, and the attempt to do so has exacted a heavy price. The horrific and ironic climax of modern civilization has been in our time what Zbigniew Brzezinski has called the "century of megadeath." Today, a wide range of issues is now forcing a reexamination and reevaluation of the significance of death.

They include questions about brain death and death with dignity, the function of hospices, alternative funerary styles and rites, and research into death and dying by writers such as Elisabeth Kübler-Ross.

We finally seem to be ready to recognize the fundamental error in our view of life and death. We are beginning to understand that death is more than the absence of life; that death, together with active life, is necessary for the formation of a larger, more essential whole. This greater whole reflects the deeper continuity of life and death that we experience as individuals and express as culture. A central challenge for the coming century will be to establish a culture based on an understanding of the relationship of life and death and of life's essential eternity. Such an attitude does not disown death but directly confronts and correctly positions it within the larger context of life.

Buddhism speaks of an intrinsic nature (*hossho* in Japanese, sometimes translated as "Dharma nature") existing within the depths of phenomenal reality. This nature depends upon and responds to environmental conditions, and it alternates between states of emergence and latency. All phenomena, including life and death, can be seen as elements within the cycle of emergence and latency, or manifestation and withdrawal.

Cycles of life and death can be likened to the alternating periods of sleep and wakefulness. Just as sleep prepares us for the next day's activity, death can be seen as a state in which we rest and replenish ourselves for new life. In this light, death should be acknowledged, along with life, as a blessing to be appreciated. The Lotus Sutra, the core of Mahayana Buddhism, states that the purpose of existence, the eternal cycles of life and death, is for living beings to "enjoy themselves at ease" (LSOC, 272). It further teaches that sustained faith and practice enable us to know a deep and abiding joy in death as well as in life, to equally "enjoy ourselves at ease" in both. Nichiren describes the attainment of this state as the "greatest of all joys" (OTT, 212).

If the tragedies of this century of war and revolution have taught us anything, it is the folly of believing that reform of external factors, such as social systems, is the linchpin to achieving happiness. I am convinced that in the coming century, the greatest emphasis must be placed on fostering inwardly directed change. In addition, our efforts must be inspired by a new understanding of life and death.

From the speech delivered at Harvard University, titled "Mahayana Buddhism and Twenty-First-Century Civilization,"[59] *Cambridge, Massachusetts, USA, September 24, 1993.*

6.6 Solidifying the State of Buddhahood in Our Lives

Stressing that those who base themselves on the Mystic Law can advance joyously in both life and death on the foundation of Buddhahood, a state of indestructible happiness, President Ikeda calls on us to establish such a state of being during our present existence.

■ Buddhism began from the quest to find a solution to the sufferings of birth, aging, sickness, and death. Life and death are the most important questions of existence, yet many people turn away from looking at them.

Nichiren Daishonin writes:

> The Nirvana Sutra states, "Human life runs its course more swiftly than a mountain stream; the person here today will not likely be here tomorrow." The Maya Sutra reads, "Imagine, for instance, a flock of sheep being driven by a chandala[60] to the slaughterhouse. Human life is exactly the same; step by step one approaches the place of death." The Lotus Sutra states, "There is no safety in the threefold world[61]; it is like a burning house, replete with a multitude of sufferings, truly to be feared" [LSOC, 105].
>
> In these passages from the sutras, our compassionate father, the World-Honored One of Great Enlightenment [Shakyamuni Buddha], admonishes us, the ordinary people of the latter age; it is his warning to us, his ignorant children. Nevertheless, the people do not awaken for even one instant; nor do they conceive a desire to attain the way for even a

> single moment. In order to decorate their bodies, which, if abandoned in the fields, would be stripped naked overnight, they spend their time striving to pile up articles of clothing.
>
> When their lives come to an end, within three days their bodies will turn into water that washes away, into dust that mixes with the earth, and into smoke that rises up into the sky, leaving no trace behind. Nevertheless, they seek to nurture these bodies and to amass great wealth. (WND-1, 891)

The Daishonin's description of human foolishness in forgetting the inevitability of death and seeking for meaningless things is just as true today as it was then—perhaps even more so. No matter how we may appear to flourish, as long as we sidestep the fundamental issue of life and death, we remain as rootless as floating weeds or like a castle built on sand.

Life is indeed impermanent—but simply being aware of its impermanence is no solution. Despairing over this reality also serves no purpose. The question is how we can create eternal value in this fleeting existence. The Lotus Sutra holds the answer.

Nichiren Daishonin describes the lives of practitioners of the Lotus Sutra very simply as follows: "Passing through the round of births and deaths, one makes one's way on the land of the Dharma nature, or enlightenment, that is inherent within oneself" (OTT, 52).

In other words, those who practice the Lotus Sutra advance serenely and steadily in both life and death on the boundless land of the Dharma nature, the firm ground of Buddhahood. They press onward in the supreme and magnificent "great white ox cart."[62]

The ground of Buddhahood is a state of indestructible happiness. It is the life state of one's own attainment of Buddhahood, as firm and solid as the earth itself. When that life state is established, it continues throughout the three existences of past, present, and future. That's why we must make our best effort in this present existence.

We advance with joy in both life and death on the earth of the Dharma nature. This means that we make our way through repeated cycles of birth and death. We advance upon the earth of our own lives, not the earth of others. That means that happiness is something we build ourselves. It is not something given to us by others. For, ultimately, things given to us by others do not last.

You may depend on your parents, but the day will come when they are no longer there. You may depend on your spouse or partner, but they may die before you. In addition, we never know what changing times will bring. For example, World War II, and the times preceding and following it, were filled with countless tragedies.

The foundation for true happiness is built through one's own efforts, one's own wisdom, one's own good fortune. The purpose of our Buddhist practice is to solidify that foundation, while our SGI activities serve to strengthen and empower us. This is the meaning of the Daishonin's words, "one makes one's way on the land of the Dharma nature" (OTT, 52).

He also says that wherever we may frolic or play, no harm will come to us; we will move about without fear like the lion king (see WND-1, 412).

We will enjoy such a state eternally—that is the aim of our Buddhist faith and practice.

We advance eternally on our own "land." When we die, we do not go either to heaven or to the depths of hell. We remain on the same land or foundation and continue to enact our drama of mission through the cycle of birth and death. We press forward along the golden path of kosen-rufu for all time.

Nichiren Daishonin urges us to keep forging ahead on the firm ground of our Buddhahood, experiencing joy in both life and death, and to continue solidifying that all-important foundation. Such is the profound view of life and death taught in Nichiren Buddhism.

From a speech delivered at a national representatives conference, Tokyo, March 29, 1996.

6.7 The Death of Someone Close to Us

Referring to Nichiren Daishonin's encouragement to Nanjo Tokimitsu and his mother, President Ikeda shares the profound insight of Buddhism for overcoming the suffering of parting with loved ones, which is one of the "eight sufferings"[63] described in Buddhism.

■ How can we overcome the inherent human sufferings of birth, aging, sickness, and death? The wisdom of Buddhism provides a sound and illuminating answer to this question.

No one can avoid the suffering of having to part from loved ones. Buddhism offers clear insights on this point.

Nanjo Hyoe Shichiro, Nanjo Tokimitsu's father, died of illness while still quite young. Tokimitsu was only seven at the time. By embracing Nichiren Daishonin's teachings, unafraid of the persecution this would invite, Hyoe Shichiro had opened the way for transforming the karma of his entire family.

In a letter of encouragement to the lay nun Ueno, Tokimitsu's mother, Nichiren writes: "When he [your deceased husband] was alive, he was a Buddha in life, and now he is a Buddha in death. He is a Buddha in both life and death" (WND-1, 456).

Life is eternal. Those who dedicate their lives to the Mystic Law are Buddhas in both life and death. Therefore, they will without fail move ahead serenely and confidently in a boundless state of being in which both life and death are filled with joy.

Carrying on her late husband's spirit, the lay nun Ueno maintained strong faith. She raised Tokimitsu and her other children to become outstanding successors who followed in their father's footsteps as sincere practitioners of Nichiren Buddhism.

It appears that Tokimitsu must have regretted losing his father at such a young age and thus missing out on receiving instruction and guidance from him.[64] Keenly aware of Tokimitsu's feelings in this regard, the Daishonin encourages and assures him:

> Persons who uphold this sutra [the Lotus Sutra], though they may be strangers to one another, will meet on Eagle Peak.[65] And how much more certain is it that you and your late father, because you both have faith in the Lotus Sutra [Nam-myoho-renge-kyo], will be reborn there together! (WND-2, 500)

Ties based on the Mystic Law are eternal. A family whose members dedicate their lives to the Mystic Law can be born together again in the same place—such is the wondrous power of the Mystic Law.

Among the Daishonin's followers was a couple who had been moved to embrace his teachings because of the death of their beloved son, the experience contributing to deepening their faith. This husband and wife earnestly practiced the Mystic Law and sincerely supported Nichiren Daishonin. In praise of their faith, Nichiren writes:

> This [the sincerity of your faith] is no ordinary matter. Indeed, Shakyamuni Buddha himself may have taken possession of

> your body. Or perhaps your deceased son has become a Buddha and, in order to guide his father and mother, has taken possession of your hearts. . . .
>
> If anything should happen to you, just as the moon emerges to shine in the dark night, so the five characters of Myoho-renge-kyo[66] will appear as a moon for you. Be convinced that Shakyamuni Buddha, the Buddhas of the ten directions, and the son who preceded you in death will appear in this moon. (WND-1, 1049–50)

Lives connected by the Mystic Law are always together, transcending the bounds of life and death, encouraging, protecting, and guiding one another as they advance on a course of absolute happiness and victory.

There is no sorrow or gloom in the realm of the Mystic Law. Family members who practice the Mystic Law will always be enveloped in the moonlight of eternity, happiness, true self, and purity—the four noble virtues of Buddhahood. Their lives will impart immeasurable hope and courage to those who follow in their footsteps.

From a speech delivered at a Tokyo No. 2 Area representatives conference, Tokyo, February 20, 2006.

6.8 Our Own Attainment of Buddhahood Enables the Deceased to Attain Buddhahood

Citing various writings of Nichiren Daishonin, President Ikeda explains the Buddhist principle that our own attainment of Buddhahood is the best and truest offering we can make for the deceased.

■ In *The Record of the Orally Transmitted Teachings,* Nichiren states:

> Now when Nichiren and his followers perform ceremonies for the deceased, reciting the Lotus Sutra and chanting Nam-myoho-renge-kyo, the ray of light from the daimoku reaches all the way to the hell of incessant suffering and makes it possible for them to attain Buddhahood then and there. This is the origin of the prayers for transference of merit for the deceased. (OTT, 17)

The power of chanting Nam-myoho-renge-kyo is unfathomable. The "light" of the daimoku we chant reaches every corner of the universe, illuminating even those agonizing in the hell of incessant suffering after death and enabling them to attain Buddhahood directly, says Nichiren Daishonin.

In "The Offering of an Unlined Robe," Nichiren writes [to the lady of Sajiki]: "Be firmly convinced that the benefits from this [your sincere offering] will extend to your parents, your grandparents, nay, even to countless living beings" (WND-1, 533). The great benefit of our Buddhist practice dedicated to kosen-rufu also flows on to the deceased as well as to unborn future generations.

Offering prayers based on the Mystic Law—chanting Nam-myoho-renge-kyo—is the best and truest offering we can make for the deceased. Because the Mystic Law has the power to help all people attain Buddhahood, not only those here in the present but throughout the three existences of past, present, and future.

The father of one of the Daishonin's disciples, Joren-bo, was a Nembutsu practitioner. In a letter to Joren-bo after his father's death, Nichiren writes: "The body that the father and mother leave behind is none other than the physical form and mind of the child.

The blessings that you, the Honorable Joren, acquire through your faith in the Lotus Sutra will lend strength to your kind father" (WND-2, 572).

Even if our parents do not practice Nichiren Buddhism, the benefit that we receive as practitioners of the Mystic Law will also become their benefit. We are alive today thanks to our parents. They gave birth to us. As such, our attainment of Buddhahood leads to their attainment of Buddhahood.

The past doesn't matter; it's the present that counts. Our ancestors' actions are not decisive; it is our actions that determine the future. All it takes is one awakened individual to shine like the sun and illuminate all of his or her family members and relations with the light of the Mystic Law.

The Daishonin notes that, without obtaining Buddhahood oneself, it would be difficult to help even one's parents attain Buddhahood, much less help other people to do so (see WND-1, 819). Let us take this insight deeply to heart.

From a speech delivered at a spring memorial service, Tokyo, March 21, 2006.

6.9 Ties Based on the Mystic Law Are Eternal

President Ikeda replies with warm encouragement to a high school division member who asks if she will ever be reunited with her beloved grandmother, who has passed away.

■ Nichiren says that we can be reunited with deceased loved ones. For example, he gently tells a mother[67] who had lost her child:

> There is a way to meet him [your deceased child] readily. With Shakyamuni Buddha as your guide, you can go to meet him in the pure land of Eagle Peak. . . . It could never happen that a woman who chants Nam-myoho-renge-kyo would fail to be reunited with her beloved child. (WND-1, 1092)

By saying that they will "meet in the pure land of Eagle Peak," the Daishonin is in effect saying, "Your child has attained Buddhahood, and you can attain Buddhahood, too, with the result that you will both be together in the same realm of Buddhahood."

This could mean that a life that has merged with the universe can feel at one with the life of another, or that two lives can meet in another Buddha land somewhere else in the universe.

Recently, it was estimated there are about 125 billion galaxies in the observable universe (according to observations with the Hubble Space Telescope by the American Astronomical Society in January 1999). But compared to the Buddhist conception of the universe, that is still far from a large number. The "Life Span" chapter that we recite during gongyo offers an even grander view of the universe, on a scale that can only be conceived as infinite. At any rate, the Earth is not the only planet inhabited by life; countless others exist.

You may be reborn with your grandmother on one of the Buddha lands among those planets. Or you may be born together on a planet where kosen-rufu is still taking place, like the Earth, and work together to aid suffering beings there. The Lotus Sutra teaches that we can be reborn freely just as we desire.

Life is eternal. Though you may be separated by death, in actuality, it is as if one of you had just gone off for a time on a trip overseas, and you couldn't meet for a while.

As a young man, President Toda lost an infant daughter. Many years later, when encouraging someone who had lost a child and asked him whether it would be possible to forge a parent-child relationship with that child again in this lifetime, he said:

> I lost my infant daughter, Yasuyo, when I was twenty-three. I held my dead child all through the night. At the time, not yet having taken faith in the Gohonzon, I was overcome with grief and fell asleep with her in my arms.
>
> And so we parted, and now I am fifty-eight. Since she was three when she died, she would now be a fine woman had she lived. Have I or have I not met my deceased daughter again in this life? This is a matter of one's own perception arising from faith. I believe that I have met her. Whether one is united with a deceased relative in this life or the next is all a matter of one's perception through faith.[68]

After Mr. Toda lost his daughter, his wife also passed away. He grieved terribly over their deaths, but he said that because he had experienced such personal loss and various other kinds of hardships he was able to encourage many others and to be a leader of the people who could understand their feelings.

Everything that happens in life has meaning. If you press ahead undefeated, through the sadness, the pain, and the feeling you can't go on, the time will come when you see its meaning. That's the power of faith, and the essence of life.

Adapted from the dialogue Discussions on Youth, *published in Japanese in September 2000.*

6.10 Sudden and Untimely Deaths

In President Ikeda's novel The New Human Revolution, *Shin'ichi Yamamoto (whose character represents President Ikeda) hastens to a regional area to encourage members after the untimely death of one of their central leaders in a car accident. He shares with them the profound perspective of life and death in Nichiren Buddhism.*

■ Throughout his writings, Nichiren Daishonin speaks of the three obstacles and four devils,[69] one of which is the hindrance of death. This devilish function serves to arouse doubt and confusion through the death of those striving diligently in Buddhist practice.

We all have our own karma, but as ordinary mortals we cannot grasp its depth. Even should steadfast practitioners of Nichiren Buddhism die young, their death will enable them to actualize the Buddhist principle of "lessening karmic retribution."[70]

Those who strive energetically for kosen-rufu as genuine practitioners of the Mystic Law are certain to attain Buddhahood, however their lives may end.

An early Buddhist scripture tells the story of a lay believer named Mahanama. He asked the Buddha where and in what form of existence he would be reborn were he to suddenly meet his end in an accident due to being distracted by the bustle of the town instead of concentrating his thoughts on the Three Treasures—the Buddha, the Law, and the Buddhist Order.

The Buddha responded, "For instance, Mahanama, if a tree bends to the east, slopes to the east, tends to the east, which way will it fall when its root is cut?"

To which Mahanama replied, "It will fall [in the direction that] it bends, slopes, and tends."[71]

Through this story, the Buddha taught that those who embrace Buddhism and practice assiduously, even if they were to meet with an unexpected, accidental death, will be carried by the Law in the direction of rebirth in good circumstances.

* * * *

Shin'ichi then began to talk about the death of Isamu Ishizaki [a central leader in Tottori Prefecture]: "There may be some members who are wondering why, given that he practiced Nichiren Buddhism, Mr. Ishizaki met with such an accident. The causes and effects inherent deep in our lives, the workings of our karma, are strict indeed. That is why, even if we practice Nichiren Buddhism, the manner of our death can occur in any number of ways.

"There may be some who die giving their lives in the struggle to uphold Buddhism, like Mr. Makiguchi who died in prison for his beliefs. There may be some who die young as a result of illness or accidents. But when viewed through the eyes of faith, it all has some extremely profound meaning.

"Those who have dedicated their lives to working for kosen-rufu are Bodhisattvas of the Earth. They are followers of the Buddha. Life is eternal. In light of the teaching of the Mystic Law, such people will absolutely attain Buddhahood. Their surviving family members will also definitely be protected. I state unequivocally that, as long as those left behind continue to persevere in faith, the good fortune and benefit accumulated through their loved ones' dedication to kosen-rufu will also pass on to them, and they will, without fail, enjoy unsurpassed happiness."

Hearing Shin'ichi's tremendous conviction, the feelings of doubt that had been clouding the members' minds evaporated and the sun of hope began to rise in their hearts.

Shin'ichi continued: "Being without a spouse or partner doesn't mean that we will never be happy. Prestige and wealth also do not guarantee happiness. True happiness, absolute happiness, is only found when we awaken to the fact that our lives embody the Mystic Law, carry out our human revolution, and manifest the great life state of Buddhahood through our Buddhist practice. We are born alone and we die alone. Only the Mystic Law has the power to protect us across the three existences of past, present, and future.

"If you continue devoting yourselves earnestly to kosen-rufu, the Buddhas and bodhisattvas throughout the ten directions and three existences will protect you. Therefore, no matter what happens, no matter what others may say or how badly they may treat you, you must never be swayed or shaken. If you become cowardly and distance yourself from faith, you will only end up miserable.

"Life is eternal, but this present lifetime flashes by in an instant. I hope you will be aware of your mission in this existence, devote yourselves to kosen-rufu, and accumulate abundant good fortune."

Adapted from The New Human Revolution, *vol. 10, "Bastion of the Pen" chapter, published in Japanese in October 2001.*

6.11 Clear Proof of Attaining Buddhahood

In this excerpt, President Ikeda discusses the final moments of those who have lived out their lives fully and without regrets through steadfast Buddhist practice.

■ Accompanied by a group of French youth division members, I once visited (in 1993) the château where Leonardo da Vinci's life came to a close.[72] These words of the Renaissance giant were engraved on a bronze plaque in the bedroom where he died: "A fulfilling life is long. As a well-spent day brings happy sleep, so a well-spent life brings happy death."

Those who have lived a good life without regrets do not fear death. How much more certain it is, then, that a life spent striving tirelessly for others and for truth and goodness, in accord with the eternal Law pervading life and the universe, will reach the summit of true joy.

Nichiren Daishonin writes:

> Continue your practice without backsliding until the final moment of your life, and when that time comes, behold! When you climb the mountain of perfect enlightenment and gaze around you in all directions, then to your amazement you will see that the entire realm of phenomena is the Land of Tranquil Light. The ground will be of lapis lazuli, and the eight paths[73] will be set apart by golden ropes. Four kinds of flowers[74] will fall from the heavens, and music will resound in the air. All Buddhas and bodhisattvas will be present in complete joy, caressed by the breezes of eternity, happiness, true self, and purity. The time is fast approaching when we too will count ourselves among their number. (WND-1, 761)

This describes the state of life—brimming with "the greatest of all joys" (OTT, 212)—found in the worlds of Buddha and bodhisattva that move in rhythm with the universe.

The Nanjo family made a lasting contribution to kosen-rufu during the Daishonin's lifetime. Nanjo Shichiro Goro, Nanjo Tokimitsu's youngest brother, died suddenly at the young age of sixteen. He was a youth of fine character and handsome appearance, and Nichiren had high hopes for his future. His mother was pregnant with him when her husband died, and she loved him deeply.

Intensely grieving Shichiro Goro's sudden death, the Daishonin repeatedly assured the Nanjo family that the deceased young man would attain Buddhahood without fail. In the postscript to one of his letters, he writes, "He [Shichiro Goro] had devoted himself to Shakyamuni Buddha and the Lotus Sutra, and he died in a fitting manner" (WND-2, 887).

Though someone may seem to have died prematurely or unexpectedly, there will be clear proof that they have attained Buddhahood. One manifestation of this is the fact that they are deeply mourned and missed by so many people. Another is the way in which the surviving family members go on to enjoy protection and prosperity. When a family carries on courageously with their lives after a loved one has passed away, the deceased continues to live on in their hearts.

Nichiren encourages Shichiro Goro's mother:

> I hope that, if you, his loving mother, are thinking with longing about your son, you will chant Nam-myoho-renge-kyo and pray to be reborn in the same place as the late Shichiro Goro and your husband, the late Nanjo.
>
> The seeds of one kind of plant are all the same; they are different from the seeds of other plants. If all of you nurture the same seeds of Myoho-renge-kyo in your hearts, then you all will be reborn together in the same land of Myoho-renge-kyo. When the three of you are reunited there face to face, how great your joy will be! (WND-1, 1074)

Based on the profound teaching of the Mystic Law, the Daishonin offers a vision of the wondrous realm of happiness stretching out before us.

Adapted from the essay series, "Thoughts on The New Human Revolution,*"*
published in Japanese in the November 3, 2000, Seikyo Shimbun.

6.12 "Illness Gives Rise to the Resolve to Attain the Way"

Referring to Nichiren Daishonin's writings, President Ikeda explains that Buddhism teaches that even illness can be an opportunity for attaining Buddhahood.

■ It is said that those who overcome a major illness deeply savor the taste of life. In Nichiren Buddhism, illness is regarded as an impetus for achieving the supreme objective of Buddhahood. The misfortune of a severe illness can become the steppingstone to a state of absolute happiness that endures for all eternity.

A famous passage from the Daishonin's writings states: "Could not this illness of your husband's be the Buddha's design, because the Vimalakirti and Nirvana sutras both teach that sick people will surely attain Buddhahood? Illness gives rise to the resolve to attain the way" (WND-1, 937). With these words, Nichiren warmly encourages a female follower whose husband is suffering from illness. This guidance conveys his boundless and freely flowing wisdom and compassion.

It is certainly true that a painful illness can motivate us to begin chanting more earnestly and abundantly than usual. Such times of suffering are precisely when we need to make the flame of our faith burn higher than ever. What matters is whether we make our illness a starting point for embarking on a course to greater happiness or the beginning of a decline toward misery.

The power of chanting Nam-myoho-renge-kyo not only produces a strong life force to help us overcome illness but also transforms the karma in the depths of our being. It elevates our inner "self" to the world of Buddhahood and enables us to attain immeasurable good fortune that leads to an indestructible state of absolute happiness.

We can then brilliantly transform the negative condition of illness beyond the neutral condition of health into a more expansive, positive condition—moving our lives in the direction of happiness. What enables us to draw forth that power is indomitable faith—faith that can courageously turn even adversity into a springboard for tremendous growth.

Of course, faith cannot immediately cure every kind of illness. Each person has their own karma, and the strength of each person's faith also differs. In addition, a struggle with illness can have a variety of profound meanings that cannot be fathomed by ordinary wisdom.

As long as we have strong faith, however, there is not the slightest doubt that we can transform our condition in the direction of health, happiness, and Buddhahood. From the perspective of life existing throughout the three existences of past, present, and future, we can move our life in the best possible direction, in the direction of happiness.

It is important to continue chanting earnestly and to keep our passionate commitment to kosen-rufu burning brightly in our hearts as long as we live. Such strong, thoroughly forged determination in faith is the primary force for serenely overcoming the sufferings of birth and death.

From a speech delivered at a Wakayama Prefecture Commemorative General Meeting, Shirahama, Wakayama Prefecture, March 24, 1988.

6.13 Changing Our Attitude Toward Aging

Introducing Shakyamuni's insight that attempting to ignore the realities of aging, sickness, and death is a form of arrogance, President Ikeda discusses the Buddhist attitude toward aging. (An excerpt on this topic from his 2013 SGI Day Peace Proposal also appears at the end of this section.)

■ In the Buddhist scriptures, Shakyamuni is said to have meditated on aging, sickness, and death and overcome three types of arrogance or pride.[75] In other words, aversion to the elderly is the arrogance of the young; aversion to the ill is the arrogance of the healthy; and aversion to the dead is the arrogance of the living.

These three types of arrogance indicated by Shakyamuni are by no means things of the past.

In discussing the problems of aging societies today, people often point to changes in society and inadequate institutions as their cause. Those are important factors, but I believe we must focus on the more essential issue of the arrogance in our hearts and work to transform human beings themselves.

People have a strong tendency to scorn or despise whatever is different from themselves. During a lecture I gave at Harvard University ("Mahayana Buddhism and Twenty-First-Century Civilization" in September 1993), I referred to this as a prejudicial mind-set, an unreasoning emphasis on individual differences. Shakyamuni described it as a single, invisible arrow piercing the hearts of the people.

By clinging to this prejudicial mind-set, we are narrowing and diminishing ourselves through our own actions. We are limiting ourselves to our present state, refusing to change.

As long as people today try to ignore the realities of aging, sickness, and death, they are rejecting their own possibilities for the future.

We need to change our attitude toward aging. The enormous life experience the elderly possess is a precious treasure—for the elderly themselves, for others around them, and for society and the world as a whole.

In one of his writings, Nichiren Daishonin notes that the long Chou dynasty of ancient China, spanning eight centuries, flourished because its founder King Wen took care of elderly people and respected their wisdom (see WND-1, 916).[76]

The words of the elderly, rich with maturity, have an often startling degree of wisdom and substance. I know many elderly people who glow with great beauty.

Those who have built an indestructible self through engaging in activities for kosen-rufu shine. Please live out your lives with self-confidence and courage.

Adapted from the dialogue, "A Discussion on the Third Stage of Life," published in Japanese in October 1998.

For further reference

In ancient India, Buddhism arose in response to the universal question of how to confront the realities of human suffering and engage with people ensnared in that suffering.

The founder of Buddhism, Gautama Buddha, or Shakyamuni, was of royal birth, which guaranteed him a life of earthly comforts. Tradition has it that his determination as a young man to abandon those comforts and seek truth through monastic practice was inspired by the "four encounters" with people afflicted by the pains of aging, sickness, and death.

But his purpose was never simply to reflect passively on life's evanescence and the inevitability of suffering. Later in life, Shakyamuni described his feelings at that time as follows: "In their foolishness, common mortals—even though they themselves will age and cannot avoid aging—when they see others aging and falling into decline, ponder it, are distressed by it, and feel shame and hate—all without ever thinking of it as their own problem," and he noted that the same holds true in our attitudes toward illness and death as well.

Shakyamuni's concern was always with the inner arrogance that allows us to objectify and isolate people confronting such sufferings as aging and illness. He was thus incapable of turning a blind eye to people suffering alone from illness or the aged cut off from the world.

There is an episode from his life that illustrates this.

One day, Shakyamuni encountered a monk who was

stricken by illness. He asked him, "Why are you suffering, and why are you alone?" The monk replied that he was lazy by nature and unable to endure the hardships associated with providing medical care to others. Thus, there was no one to tend to him. At which Shakyamuni responded, "Good man, I will look after you." Shakyamuni took the stricken monk outdoors, changed his soiled bedding, washed him, and dressed him in new clothes. He then firmly encouraged him to always be diligent in his religious practice. The monk was immediately restored to a state of physical and mental well-being and joy.

In my view, it was not just Shakyamuni's unexpected and devoted care that affected the monk in this way. Rather, the fact that Shakyamuni encouraged him using the same strict yet warm language that he used with other, healthy disciples revived the flame of dignity that was so close to being extinguished in this man's life.

This story as I have outlined it so far is based on an account in *The Great Tang Dynasty Record of the Western Regions.* However, when we compare this to the version transmitted in other sutras, a further aspect of Shakyamuni's motivation comes to light.

After having tended to the sick monk, Shakyamuni is said to have gathered the other monks and asked them what they knew about the man's condition. As it turned out, they had been aware of his illness and the gravity of his condition, and yet none among them had made any effort to provide care.

The Buddha's disciples answered in terms almost identical to those of the ailing monk: he had never attended to any of them in their time of illness, and so they refrained from attending to him.

This corresponds to the logic of personal responsibility as it is often used in contemporary settings to negate the need to care for others. For the ailing monk, this attitude fostered feelings of resignation, and for the other disciples it manifested itself as an arrogant justification of their disinterest. This logic atrophied his spirit and clouded theirs.

"Whoever would tend to me, should tend to the sick." With these words, Shakyamuni sought to dispel the delusions clouding the minds of his disciples and spur them to a correct understanding.

In other words, practicing the Buddha's way means to actively share the joys and sufferings of others—never turning one's back on those who are troubled and in distress, being moved by others' experiences as if they were one's own. Through such efforts, not only do those directly afflicted by suffering regain their sense of dignity, but so too do those who empathetically embrace that suffering.

The inherent dignity of life does not manifest in isolation. Rather, it is through our active engagement with others that their unique and irreplaceable nature becomes evident. At the same time, the determination to protect that dignity against all incursions adorns and brings forth the luster of our own lives.

By asserting an essential equality between himself and an ailing monk, the Buddha sought to awaken people to the fact that the value of human life is undiminished by illness or age: he refused to acknowledge such distinctions and discriminations. In this sense, to regard the sufferings of others due to illness or age as evidence of defeat or failure in life is not only an error in judgment but undermines the dignity of all concerned.

The philosophical foundation of the Soka Gakkai

International is the teachings of Nichiren (1222–82), who emphasized the supremacy of the Lotus Sutra which, he stated, marks the epitome of Shakyamuni's enlightenment. In the Lotus Sutra, a massive jeweled tower arises from within the earth to symbolize the dignity and value of life. Nichiren compared the four sides of the treasure tower to the "four aspects" of birth, aging, sickness, and death,[77] asserting that we can confront the stark realities of aging, illness, and even death in such a way that we remain undefeated by the suffering that accompanies them. We can make these experiences—normally only seen in a negative light—the impetus for a more richly dignified and valuable way of living.

The dignity of life is not something separate from the inevitable trials of human existence, and we must engage actively with others, sharing their suffering and exerting ourselves to the last measure of our strength, if we are to open a path toward authentic happiness for both ourselves and others.

From SGI President Ikeda's Peace Proposal "Building a Global Society of Peace and Creative Coexistence," commemorating the 38th SGI Day, January 26, 2013.

6.14 Transforming the Sufferings of Birth and Death

President Ikeda stresses the importance of Buddhist practice to accumulate the treasures of the heart in this existence in order to transcend the sufferings of birth and death and achieve a life state of eternal happiness.

■ According to a Buddhist story, seven elder Brahmans once traveled from afar to visit Shakyamuni. Though they had made the long trip to learn about the Buddhist teachings from him, they spent their days in the lodging where they were staying, engaged in idle conversation, laughing and amusing themselves.

Shakyamuni came to see them and said: "All beings rely on five things. What are the five? One, they rely on their youth. Two, they rely on their upright appearance. Three, they rely on their great strength. Four, they rely on their wealth. Five, they rely on their noble family. While you, seven sirs, are speaking in a low tone or loudly laughing, what do you rely on?"[78]

Shakyamuni then went on to tell them that life is uncertain and fleeting, characterized by the four sufferings of birth, aging, sickness, and death. Hearing Shakyamuni, the seven Brahmans realized for the first time what they should be doing and began to strive seriously in their practice.

"What do you rely on?" Shakyamuni asked. In other words, what sustains you in this life?

Nichiren Daishonin teaches three treasures in life: the treasures of the storehouse, the treasures of the body, and the treasures of the heart (see WND-1, 851).

The five things that all beings rely on in the story all correspond to the treasures of the storehouse or the treasures of the body. Wealth, of course, corresponds to the treasures of the storehouse. Youth, beauty, health, and ability, along with social status, correspond to the treasures of the body. All of these things have value in life, and it may be natural, in that respect, for us to pursue them. But the question is whether they are really genuine treasures in life that can offer eternal sustenance.

Let me give some concrete examples. Some people are harmed or killed for their wealth. Those who are physically attractive may be envied or exploited by others. Fame and power can lead people to become arrogant and ruin their lives, and there are many of high social position who allow themselves to be seduced by the devilish nature of power, to their own undoing. None of these so-called treasures continue forever.

As such, the treasures of the storehouse and the treasures of the body are not genuine sustenance that can provide true happiness. On their own, they cannot enable us to lead a life of real fulfillment.

What do we need to live such a life? Nichiren tells us, "The treasures of the heart are the most valuable of all" (WND-1, 851).

The treasures of the heart refer to faith in the Mystic Law. Faith is the eternal treasure and sustenance of human life. It encompasses immeasurable benefit and boundless good fortune. Its power is as vast as the universe and can transform our entire environment or world. It is the source of inexhaustible joy and immense wisdom and compassion, enabling us to employ the treasures of the storehouse and the treasures of the body to attain eternal happiness.

Each of you already possesses this supreme sustenance of life. All you have to do is tap its limitless power.

Life is brief. Youth passes by in a flash, easily wasted in indecision, complaining, criticizing others, or being defeated by one's own laziness. Every day is precious.

I hope you will spend your youth in a fulfilling manner, leading strong lives in the real world and at the same time contemplating the vast universe, pondering eternity, and making each day worth a thousand years, a thousand eons.

From a speech delivered at an Okinawa Prefecture youth division representatives training course, Okinawa, February 19, 1988.

Notes

Chapter 1

1. Translated from Thai. *Ngeakhit khamkhom lea khamuayphon* (Thai Proverbs and Maxims), complied and edited by Anusorn (Bangkok: Ruamsan, 1993), 207.
2. Translated from Japanese. Josei Toda, *Toda Josei zenshu* (Collected Writings of Josei Toda) (Tokyo: Seikyo Shimbunsha, 1989), 4,:257–59. (Guidance given at the West Japan Joint Chapter General Meeting held on January 23, 1955.)
3. This is the revised translation based on the English translation of the Lotus Sutra as it appears in *The Lotus Sutra and Its Opening and Closing Sutras.* According to the Soka Gakkai Buddhist Scripture Translation Department, these revisions will be incorporated in a future revised edition of *The Record of the Orally Transmitted Teachings.*
4. By Japanese author Fumiko Hayashi (1903–51).

Chapter 2

5. John Milton, *Paradise Lost,* ed. Christopher Ricks (London: Penguin Books, 1989), 12.
6. *Amrita:* A legendary, ambrosia-like liquid. In ancient India, it was regarded as the sweet-tasting beverage of the gods. In China, it was thought to rain down from heaven when the world became peaceful. Amrita is said to remove sufferings and give immortality. The word *amrita* means immortality and is often translated as sweet dew.
7. Land of Eternally Tranquil Light: Also, Land of Tranquil Light. The

Buddha land, which is free from impermanence and impurity. In many sutras, the actual saha world in which human beings dwell is described as an impure land filled with delusions and sufferings, while the Buddha land is described as a pure land free from these and far removed from this saha world. In contrast, the Lotus Sutra reveals the saha world to be the Buddha land, or the Land of Eternally Tranquil Light, and explains that the nature of a land is determined by the minds of its inhabitants.

8. Fusion of reality and wisdom: The fusion of the objective reality or truth and the subjective wisdom to realize that truth. Here, it refers to our lives (wisdom) fusing with the Gohonzon (reality or truth), and attaining enlightenment or Buddhahood.
9. Translated from Japanese. Josei Toda, *Toda Josei zenshu* (Collected Works of Josei Toda) (Tokyo: Seikyo Shimbunsha, 1982), 2:446–47.
10. The word Gohonzon is formed in Japanese by appending the honorific prefix *go* to the word *honzon,* object of fundamental respect or devotion. In Nichiren Buddhism, it refers specifically to the object of devotion established by Nichiren Daishonin.
11. Six stages of practice: Also, six identities. Six stages in the practice of the Lotus Sutra formulated by the Great Teacher T'ien-t'ai in his *Great Concentration and Insight.* They are as follows: (1) The stage of being a Buddha in theory; (2) the stage of hearing the name and words of the truth; (3) the stage of perception and action; (4) the stage of resemblance to enlightenment; (5) the stage of progressive awakening; (6) the stage of ultimate enlightenment, or the highest stage of practice.
12. Translated from Japanese. Josei Toda, *Toda Josei zenshu* (Collected Works of Josei Toda) (Tokyo: Seikyo Shimbunsha, 1992), 6:608. (Lecture on "The Real Aspect of the Gohonzon," March 6, 1956.)
13. The Japanese word for faith (*shinjin*) consists of two Chinese characters.
14. The full quote from "The Object of Devotion for Observing the Mind" reads: "Showing profound compassion for those unable to comprehend the gem of the doctrine of three thousand realms in a single moment of life, the Buddha wrapped it within the five characters [of Myoho-renge-kyo], with which he then adorned the necks of the ignorant people of the latter age" (WND-1, 376). Myoho-renge-kyo is written with five Chinese characters, while Nam-myoho-renge-kyo is written with seven (*nam,* or *namu,* being comprised of two characters). The Daishonin often uses Myoho-renge-kyo synonymously with Nam-myoho-renge-kyo in his writings.

15. Translated from Japanese. Nichikan, *Kanjin no Honzon-sho mondan* (Commentary on "The Object of Devotion for Observing the Mind"), in *Nichikan Shonin mondan-shu* (The Commentaries of Nichikan Shonin) (Tokyo: Seikyo Shimbunsha, 1980), 548.
16. Six sense organs: Also, six sensory organs. The eyes, ears, nose, tongue, body, and mind. The contact of the six sense organs with their corresponding six objects gives rise to the six consciousnesses—sight, hearing, smell, taste, touch, and thought.
17. Nichikan, *Kanjin no Honzon-sho mondan* (Commentary on "The Object of Devotion for Observing the Mind"), 472.
18. "Ten thousand" here means "all" or "innumerable."

Chapter 3

19. The Japanese word *gongyo* literally means "assiduous practice."
20. Nichiren Daishonin notes that the Great Teacher Miao-lo of China writes in *The Annotations on "Great Concentration and Insight"*: "One understands that everything that is contained within this body of ours is modeled after heaven and earth. . . . The breath going in and out of the nose imitates the wind passing over the mountain lakes and stream valleys, the breath going in and out of the mouth imitates the wind in the open sky. The eyes correspond to the sun and moon, and their opening and closing correspond to day and night. The hairs of the head are like the stars and constellations, . . . the veins like the rivers and streams, the bones like the rocks, the skin and flesh like the earth, and the body hairs like the thickets and groves of trees" (WND-2, 848–49).
21. Toki Jonin (1216–99): A lay follower of Nichiren Daishonin. He lived in Wakamiya, Katsushika District of Shimosa Province (part of present-day Chiba Prefecture) and was a leading samurai retainer of Lord Chiba, the constable of that province. He converted to the Daishonin's teaching around 1254, the year after it was first proclaimed at Seicho-ji, a temple in Kominato of Awa Province. Also known as the lay priest Toki, he was the recipient of many of the Daishonin's writings, including "The Object of Devotion for Observing the Mind," the majority of which he carefully preserved.
22. The sixty-six provinces refer to the entire country of ancient Japan.
23. Myoho-renge-kyo is written with five Chinese characters, while Nam-myoho-renge-kyo is written with seven (*nam*, or *namu*, being composed

of two characters). The Daishonin often uses Myoho-renge-kyo synonymously with Nam-myoho-renge-kyo in his writings.

24. From a commentary by Fu Ta-shih.
25. Bodhisattvas of the Earth: An innumerable host of bodhisattvas who emerge from beneath the earth and to whom Shakyamuni Buddha entrusts the propagation of the Mystic Law, or the essence of the Lotus Sutra, in the Latter Day of the Law. They are described in "Emerging from the Earth," the fifteenth chapter of the Lotus Sutra, the first chapter of the sutra's essential teaching (latter fourteen chapters).
26. Major world system: Also, thousand-millionfold world. One of the world systems described in ancient Indian cosmology.
27. "Ten thousand" here means "all" or "innumerable."
28. Seven kinds of treasures: Also, the seven treasures. Seven precious substances. The list differs among the Buddhist scriptures. In the Lotus Sutra, the seven are gold, silver, lapis lazuli, seashell, agate, pearl, and carnelian.
29. Purification of the six sense organs: Also, purification of the six senses. This refers to the six sense organs of eyes, ears, nose, tongue, body, and mind becoming pure, making it possible to apprehend all things correctly. "Benefits of the Teacher of the Law," the nineteenth chapter of the Lotus Sutra, explains that those who uphold and practice the sutra acquire 800 benefits of the eyes, nose and body, and 1,200 benefits of the ears, tongue, and mind, and that through these benefits the six sense organs become refined and pure.
30. Vapor condenses on a mirror placed outside at night. It was said that the mirror drew this water down from the moon.
31. Nichiren Daishonin writes: "As life does not go beyond the moment, the Buddha expounded the blessings that come from a single moment of rejoicing [on hearing the Lotus Sutra]. If two or three moments were required, this could no longer be called the original vow of the Buddha endowed with great impartial wisdom, the single vehicle of the teaching that directly reveals the truth and leads all living beings to attain Buddhahood" (WND-1, 62).

Chapter 4

32. William Shakespeare, *As You Like It*, in *The Complete Works, Illustrated* (New York: Gramercy Books, 1975), Act II, Scene 7. 239.

33. Maxim Gorky, *The Lower Depths: Unabridged,* trans. Jennie Covan and ed. Julie Nord (Toronto: Dover Publications, Inc., 2000), 5.
34. Sir Walter Scott, *Rob Roy,* ed. Ian Duncan (New York: Oxford University Press, 2008), 211.
35. Five components: Also, five components of life. They consist of form, perception, conception, volition, and consciousness. Buddhism holds that these constituent elements unite temporarily to form an individual living being. Together they also constitute one of the three realms of existence, the other two being the realm of living beings and the realm of the environment.
36. This famous parable about a woman named Kisa Gotami appears in the *Therigatha Atthakatha* (Commentary to the *Therigatha*).
37. True cause: Also, mystic principle of the true cause. Nichiren Buddhism directly expounds the true cause for enlightenment as Nam-myoho-renge-kyo, which is the Law of life and the universe. It teaches a way of Buddhist practice of always moving forward from this moment on based on this fundamental Law.
38. Nichiren Daishonin writes: "Shakyamuni's practices and the virtues he consequently attained are all contained within the five characters of Myoho-renge-kyo. If we believe in these five characters, we will naturally be granted the same benefits as he was" (WND-1, 365).
39. Leo Tolstoy, *Tolstoy's Diaries,* ed. and trans. R. F. Christian (London: The Athlone Press, 1985), 1:264. (September 15, 1889)
40. Ten demon daughters: The ten female protective deities who appear in "Dharani," the twenty-sixth chapter of the Lotus Sutra, as the "daughters of *rakshasa* demons" or the "ten rakshasa daughters." They vow to the Buddha to guard and protect the sutra's votaries.
41. Nichiren Daishonin had been pardoned the previous year, in March 1274, and was residing at Minobu when he wrote this letter, "Winter Always Turns to Spring," dated May 1275.
42. The Nirvana Sutra says: "They may be poorly clad and poorly fed, seek wealth in vain, be born to an impoverished and lowly family or one with erroneous views, or be persecuted by their sovereign. They may be subjected to various other sufferings and retributions. It is due to the blessings obtained by protecting the Law that they can diminish in this lifetime their suffering and retribution" (WND-1, 497).
43. Lessening karmic retribution: This term, which literally means, "transforming the heavy and receiving it lightly," appears in the Nirvana Sutra.

"Heavy" indicates negative karma accumulated over countless lifetimes in the past. As a benefit of protecting the correct teaching of Buddhism, we can experience relatively light karmic retribution in this lifetime, thereby expiating heavy karma that ordinarily would adversely affect us not only in this lifetime, but over many lifetimes to come.

Chapter 5

44. Translated from Japanese. Josei Toda, *Toda Josei zenshu* (Collected Writings of Josei Toda) (Tokyo: Seikyo Shimbunsha, 1984), 4:378.
45. The three bodies of the Buddha refer to the Dharma body, the reward body, and the manifested body. The Dharma body is the fundamental truth, or Law, to which a Buddha is enlightened. The reward body is the wisdom to perceive the Law. And the manifested body is the compassionate action the Buddha carries out to lead people to happiness.
46. Translated from Japanese. Shin'yu Iwano, ed. *Agonbu* (The Chinese Versions of the Agamas), in *Kokuyaku issaikyo* (The Japanese Translation of the Complete Chinese Buddhist Canon), (Tokyo: Daito Shuppansha, 1969), 9–10:152. (Ekottarāgama 38.5)
47. Ibid.
48. Based on the Japanese text of President Ikeda's dialogue with Brazilian Academy of Letters president Austregésilo de Athayde: *Nijuisseiki no jinken o kataru* (A Dialogue on Human Rights in the Twenty-first Century) (Tokyo: Ushio Shuppansha, 1995).
49. Translated from Japanese. Tatsuo Morimoto, *Ganji to Tagoru* (Gandhi and Tagore) (Tokyo: Daisanbunmei-sha, 1995), 116–17.
50. Ibid., 117.

Chapter 6

51. Daisaku Ikeda, "Mahayana Buddhism and Twenty-first-Century Civilization," *A New Humanism: The University Addresses of Daisaku Ikeda* (New York: Weatherhill, 1995), 153.
52. Great white ox cart: A carriage adorned with jewels and drawn by a great white ox. It appears in the parable of the three carts and the burning house in "Simile and Parable," the third chapter of the Lotus Sutra, where it represents the one Buddha vehicle, or the supreme vehicle of Buddhahood.

53. In a portion of the speech not included in this excerpt, President Ikeda cited the passage from Nichiren Daishonin's writing "On the Large Carriages Drawn by White Oxen": "These large carriages drawn by white oxen [i.e., the great white ox carts] are able to fly at will through the sky of the essential nature of phenomena [Dharma nature, or enlightenment]. Those persons who come after me will ride in these carriages and journey to [the pure land of] Eagle Peak. And I, Nichiren, riding in the same kind of carriage, will come out to greet them" (WND-2, 976).
54. Four noble truths: A fundamental doctrine of Buddhism clarifying the cause of suffering and the way of emancipation. The four noble truths are the truth of suffering, the truth of the origin of suffering, the truth of the cessation of suffering, and the truth of the path to the cessation of suffering. Shakyamuni is said to have expounded the four noble truths at Deer Park in Varanasi, India, during his first sermon after attaining enlightenment. They are: (1) all existence is suffering; (2) suffering is caused by selfish craving; (3) the eradication of selfish craving brings about the cessation of suffering and enables one to attain nirvana; and (4) there is a path by which this eradication can be achieved, namely, the discipline of the eightfold path. The eightfold path consists of right views, right thinking, right speech, right action, right way of life, right endeavor, right mindfulness, and right meditation.
55. In the Lotus Sutra, Shakyamuni declares that his life as a Buddha is eternal, but as a means to help living beings arouse a seeking spirit, he appears to enter nirvana, or extinction.
56. Based on the Japanese text of President Ikeda's book titled *Seimei o kataru*.
57. In *The Record of the Orally Transmitted Teachings,* Nichiren Daishonin says, "We may also say that nonexistence (*mu*) and existence (*u*), birth and death, ebbing and flowing, existing in this world and entering extinction, are all, every one of them, actions of the eternally abiding inherent nature" (OTT, 127–28).
58. Translated from Japanese. Leo Tolstoy, *Torusutoi zenshu* (Collected Works of Tolstoy) (Tokyo: Iwanami Shoten, 1931), 21:408.
59. Daisaku Ikeda, "Mahayana Buddhism and Twenty-first-Century Civilization," *A New Humanism: The University Addresses of Daisaku Ikeda* (New York: Weatherhill, 1995), 151–53.
60. Chandala: A class of untouchables, below the lowest of the four castes in the ancient Indian caste system. People in this class handled corpses,

butchered animals and carried out other tasks associated with death or the killing of living things. Nichiren declared himself to be a member of the chandala class because he was born to a fisherman's family.

61. Threefold world: The world of unenlightened beings who transmigrate within the six paths (from hell through the realm of heavenly beings). The threefold world consists of, in ascending order, the world of desire, the world of form, and the world of formlessness. In a general sense, it refers to the saha world in which we dwell.
62. In the writing "The Large Carriage Drawn by a White Ox," Nichiren Daishonin states: "This carriage [the great white ox cart] I have been describing has the two doctrines, the theoretical teaching and the essential teaching, as its wheels, and it is hitched to the ox of Myoho-renge-kyo. It is a carriage that goes round and round in the cycle of birth and death, birth and death, in the burning house that is the threefold world. But with the linchpin of a believing mind [to keep the wheels in place] and the oil of determination applied to them, it can carry one to the pure land of Eagle Peak. Or again, we might say that the mind king acts as the ox, while birth and death are like the wheels. The Great Teacher Dengyo states, 'The two phases of life and death are the wonderful workings of one mind. The two ways of existence and nonexistence are the true functions of an inherently enlightened mind.' And T'ien-t'ai says, 'The ten factors are [the true aspect of the Lotus and also the reality of the carriage drawn by a white ox] . . . the ultimate realm is the true aspect of life'" (WND-2, 723–24).
63. Eight sufferings: They are the four sufferings of birth, aging, sickness, and death, plus the suffering of having to part from those whom one loves, the suffering of having to meet with those whom one hates, the suffering of being unable to obtain what one desires, and the suffering arising from the five components that constitute one's body and mind.
64. Nichiren writes: "You lost your father at a very early age, and hence were deprived of his instruction and guidance. When I think of what this must have meant for you, I cannot restrain my tears" (WND-2, 500).
65. Eagle Peak, or the pure land of Eagle Peak, is a term symbolizing the eternal state of Buddhahood.
66. Myoho-renge-kyo is written with five Chinese characters, while Nam-myoho-renge-kyo is written with seven (*nam*, or *namu*, being comprised of two characters). Nichiren Daishonin, however, often uses

Myoho-renge-kyo synonymously with Nam-myoho-renge-kyo in his writings.

67. Written to the lay nun Ueno, the mother of Nanjo Tokimitsu, upon the sudden death of Tokimitsu's youngest brother, Shichiro Goro.
68. Translated from Japanese. Josei Toda, *Toda Josei zenshu* (Collected Writings of Josei Toda) (Tokyo: Seikyo Shimbunsha, 1982), 2:174.
69. Three obstacles and four devils: Various obstacles and hindrances to the practice of Buddhism. The three obstacles are (1) the obstacle of earthly desires, (2) the obstacle of karma, and (3) the obstacle of retribution. The four devils are (1) the hindrance of the five components, (2) the hindrance of earthly desires, (3) the hindrance of death, and (4) the hindrance of the devil king.
70. Lessening karmic retribution: This term, which literally means, "transforming the heavy and receiving it lightly," appears in the Nirvana Sutra. "Heavy" indicates negative karma accumulated over countless lifetimes in the past. As a benefit of protecting the correct teaching of Buddhism, we can experience relatively light karmic retribution in this lifetime, thereby expiating heavy karma that ordinarily would adversely affect us not only in this lifetime, but over many lifetimes to come.
71. *The Book of the Kindred Sayings (Sanyutta-Nikāya) or Grouped Suttas, Part 5*, trans. Mrs. Rhys Davids (Oxford: Pali Text Society, 1994), 321.
72. Le Clos-Lucé, formerly the castle of Cloux, near Amboise, France; it is now a Leonardo da Vinci museum.
73. The eight paths lead in eight directions, that is, toward the eight points of the compass.
74. Mandarava, great mandarava, manjushaka, and great manjushaka flowers. Fragrant red and white flowers that, according to Indian tradition, bloom in heaven.
75. See "The Book of Threes," in *The Book of the Gradual Sayings (Anguttara-Nikaya) or More- Numbered Suttas*, trans. F. L. Woodward (Oxford: Pali Text Society, 1995), 1:129–30.
76. The Daishonin writes: "King Wen of the Chou dynasty was victorious in battle because he took care to provide for elderly people. During the thirty-seven reigns spanning eight hundred years in which his descendants ruled, there were some incidents of misgovernment, but on the whole the Chou dynasty prospered due to that fundamental virtue" (WND-1, 916).

77. See OTT, 90.
78. *The Scriptural Text: Verses of the Doctrine, with Parables,* trans. Charles Willemen from the Chinese of Fa-li and Fa-chü (Taisho Volume 4, Number 211) (Berkeley, CA: Numata Center for Buddhist Translation and Research, 1999), 116.

Index